2016 Edit

Though the author and editors of this book have made every effort to ensure accuracy and completeness, we assume no responsibility for any errors, inaccuracies, omissions or inconsistencies.

To submit comments, concerns, questions or feedback regarding this exam please visit http://www.medicalbillingandmedicalcoding.com/contactus.html.

We would also like express our gratitude to:

- MTsamples.com, for the use of their dictation and operative notes.
- The ASC review, for their coding guidance article by the American Medical Association.
- Ingenix for the insight and guidance provided in their "Coder's Desk Reference" and their ICD-10-CM Expert Edition manual.
- The AMA, for their valuable insights provided in the CPT Professional Edition manual.
- The members and experts in the AAPC forums, who continually hand out out quality professional coding advice.
- The AAPC Local Norwalk Chapter in Ohio for providing their advice, insight and time proofreading and editing the exam.

Thank you!

Table of Contents

Scantron Bubble Sheets

Congratulations!

You have taken a major step toward your CPC certification.

This 150-question CPC practice exam has been constructed to mirror the actual CPC exam. You will find that each question and its answer closely resemble those on the actual CPC exam. The layout of this exam is the layout that you can expect to see on exam day.

For the best results we suggest the following:

1. Read through the CPC Exam Study Guide in its entirety, including the Common Anatomy Terms and Medical Terminology handouts included after the Study Guide.
2. Read and study this entire packet prior to starting the CPC practice exam.
3. Locate the Scantron Bubble Sheets, where you will mark your answers to the 150 questions.
4. Read the Proctor-to-Coder Instructions just prior to taking the exam.
5. When taking the exam, set aside 5 hours and 40 minutes in a quiet, distraction-free environment and try to take the exam in one sitting.
6. Have two or three sharpened #2 pencils, an eraser, a sheet of scrap paper, a calculator, your three coding manuals and the CPC practice exam.
7. Take a long break before trying to grade the exam and comprehend the rationale. You may want to have someone else grade the answers and give you your results, and sit down with the rationale later.

The idea is to create a practice environment that simulates the actual CPC exam. That way you will not feel flustered or overwhelmed when taking the test for real – you will recognize the setting and realize your goal: Passing the CPC.

The first step in exam preparation is knowing and rechecking your coding manuals. Since the majority of the CPC exam is focused on the CPT coding manual, we will focus on this manual during preparation.

CPT Manual:

Front Cover: Common coding conventions (symbols) are listed here, along with coding modifiers with a short descriptions. HCPCS modifiers that are approved for CPT Level I use are also listed, with a short description.

Introduction: Introductions are located a few pages in from the front cover and labeled with Roman numerals rather than page numbers. The introduction should be read at least once. Highlighting and notations are allowed and encouraged.

References: Following the introduction there are a few pages with common medical prefixes, suffixes, root words, directions, positions and anatomical terms. This page should be tabbed for easy use during the exam. Terms not already listed on these pages can be written in by hand. Using the common medical anatomy terms and medical terminology handouts provided with this packet, transfer unknown terms to these pages in your CPT book.

After the common terminology pages, there are a few pages that list where anatomical illustrations may be found in your CPT manual. This is followed by three diagrams of the body planes and aspects. The location of these pages should also be noted (or tabbed).

General Layout: The CPT manual is divided into chapters that are organ system specific (e.g. Integumentary, Respiratory, etc.) Chapters are listed in numerical order, with the exception of E/M codes, which start with 99. Each chapter has chapter-specific coding guidelines listed prior to their code sets. The general coding guidelines for each chapter should be read at least once. Highlighting and notations are allowed and suggested. Avoid highlighting common words and phrases and try to highlight specific guidelines and rules.

Following general coding guidelines are the codes sets, which may or may not have code-specific coding guidelines.

Code sets are generally listed in anatomical order. This means that codes pertaining to the outside of the body are listed first and progress inward, and codes pertaining to the top of the body are listed first and progress downward. Example: in the respiratory system the codes pertaining to the nose start with the out-side of the nose (skin) and progress inward, eventually to the sinuses (outside inward). Codes pertaining to the nose are all listed before codes pertaining to the lungs (top to bottom). Each chapter follows this basic layout.

General Coding Rules: All CPT codes have a common descriptor, a unique descriptor or both. A common descriptor is a description that applies to more than one CPT code and is located prior to the semi-colon (;). The unique descriptor is a description that applies to a single CPT code and is located after the semi-colon (;).

Unique descriptors are indented beneath a common descriptor beside their CPT code.

Example:

12001 Simple repair of a superficial wound of scalp, neck, axillae, external genitalia, trunk and/or extremities (including hands and feet); 2.5cm or less

12002	2.6cm to 7.5cm
12004	7.6cm to 12.5cm

CPT codes may also have notations beneath them indicating specific coding guidelines, such as a code with which it may not be used in conjunction, sequencing, etc.

Coding conventions may be located to the left of a CPT code, also indicating a specific coding guideline. A short description of the convention's meaning may be found at the bottom of each page and a full description can be found in the introduction at the beginning of the CPT manual.

Following the chapters that contain category I codes are two indicies containing category II and category III codes. Category II codes are tracking codes used for performance and quality measures. Category III codes end in the letter T and are temporary codes used for new and emerging technology, services and procedures. Following the category II and III codes are appendices A – N. Each appendix is useful in its own way, but for the examination we suggest reading and knowing the locations of appendix A (modifiers and their full descriptions and guidelines), appendix D (a list of all add-on codes), appendix E (a list of all modifier 51- exempt codes), appendix F (modifier 63-exempt codes), appendix G (codes that include conscious sedation), appendix K (codes with products pending FDA approval), appendix L (vascular families) and appendix N (a list of re-sequenced codes). Following the appendices is the alphabetic index.

The back cover of the CPT manual contains common medical abbreviations.

General coding guidelines should follow the introduction and chapter-specific coding guidelines should follow general coding guidelines.

ICD-10-CM Manual

ICD-10-CM manuals vary, depending on the publisher, but all should contain an introduction in the beginning of the manual. The introduction should contain steps to correct coding, including convention descriptions and proper usage.

Important things to know regarding ICD-10-CM conventions and coding guidelines include (but are not limited to):

- Meanings of NEC and NOS
- Definitions and proper use of brackets [ ], parentheses ( ) and colons :
- Proper use of the following notations:
    - o Includes
    - o Excludes1 and Excludes2
    - o "other specified" codes
    - o "unspecified" codes
    - o "Code first"
    - o "use additional code"
    - o "in diseases classified elsewhere"
    - o "and"
    - o "with"
    - o "see" and "see also"
- You must always report and utilize a code at its highest number of characters available. ICD-10-CM codes are composed of 3, 4, 5, 6 or 7 characters. A code is invalid if it has not been coded to the full number of characters required for that code, including the 7th character, if applicable.
- Rules regarding:
    - o Signs and Symptoms
    - o Coding Manifestations
    - o Code Sequencing
    - o Combination Coding
    - o Coding Sequela (Late Effects)
    - o Coding Laterality
- Always verify a code in the tabular index.
- Read three-digit category coding guidelines and look for code specific coding guidelines and notations beneath specific codes.

Things to Remember

- Diagnostic endoscopies that turn into procedural endoscopies become bundled with the procedural code and cannot be coded separately.
- Modifier 51 is generally added to all secondary procedure codes unless the code is modifier 51 exempt.
- Modifiers are not appended to ICD-10-CM codes, only to CPT (level I) and HCPCS (level II) codes. The external causes of morbidity codes (V00-Y99) should never be sequenced as the first-listed or principal diagnosis.

- Assign the external cause code, with the appropriate 7th character (initial encounter, subsequent encounter or sequela) for each encounter for which the injury or condition is being treated.
- Factors influencing health status and contact with health service (Z00-Z99) are for use in any healthcare setting, and may be used as either a first-listed or secondary code, depending on the circumstances of the encounter.
- "Probable," "Suspected," "Rule Out" and similarly worded diagnoses should not be coded in an outpatient setting.

General Test Taking Tips

- Answer the easy questions first and skip the long ones. Each question is worth the same numbernumbernumber of points, and the long ones take more time to read. Also remember to skip the answer on the bubble sheet.
- Start the exam with the chapter in which you are most knowledgeable, even if that means starting in the middle of the exam.
- Skip using the alphabetic index during the exam. Instead, take the four answers that are provided to you and look them up directly in the tabular index.
- Follow your first instinct. Statistics show that when an individual comes back to a previously answered question and changes the answer, he or she often had the correct answer and changed it to an incorrect one.
- At some point, everyone runs into a question that he or she does not know how to answer. Never leave an question blank, because even a guess will give you a 25% chance of getting the correct answer.
- When making a guess, try to make an educated one, based on logic.
  - Often the correct answer (code) will be repeated in at least two of the four options. An answer with a code that does not appear in any of the other options can often be ruled out.
  - The answer often corresponds to the chapter that is being tested. For example, if you are in the "respiratory" chapter questions, the answer will most likely contain a 30000 code. Answers that have codes from other chapters (e.g. A digestive code; 50000 series) can most likely be ruled out.
  - Often, a modifier will be appended to two of the four options. If you can determine if the modifier is appropriate, you can usually narrow down your options from four to two, giving you a 50% chance of guessing the correct answer.

- According to the AAPC Exam Proctors Sheet, which is distributed by the AAPC to the exam proctors, *tabs can be inserted, taped, pasted, glued or stapled in the manuals, if the obvious intent is to earmark a page with words or numbers and not add supplemental information. No other material of any kind may be taped stapled or glued into the manuals to be used during the examination. Handwritten notes in coding books (as those commonly seen in daily work coding activities) are permitted. Manuals will not be disqualified due to writing contained therein.*
  - o Additional anatomy labels, such as those on the provided diagrams, are useful. An example would be to label the Incus, Malleus and Stapes (in the auditory system) with their common names: Anvil, Hammer and Stirrup.

Directional Terms:

Anterior (ventral) - Toward the front of the body

Central - At or near the center of the body or organ

Distal - Part of an extremity that is farther from the point of attachment to the trunk

External (superficial) - Toward or on the surface of the body

Inferior (caudad) - Away from the head

Internal - Away from the surface of the body

Lateral - Away from the midline of the body

Medial - Toward the midline of the body

Parietal - Pertaining to the outer boundary of body cavities

Peripheral - External to or away from the center of the body or organ

Posterior (dorsal) - Toward the back of the body

Proximal - Part of an extremity that is closer to the point of attachment to the trunk

Superior (cephalad) - Toward the head

Visceral - Pertaining to the internal organs

Planes:

Frontal Plane - (e.g. Coronal Plane) is an imaginary line that runs vertically across the shoulders, sides and hips to divide the body from front to back.

Midsagittal Plane - (e.g. Sagittal Plane or Lateral Plane) is an imaginary line that runs vertically down the spine, face and center of the abdomen to divide the body into left and right portions.

Transverse Plane - (e.g. Cross-Sectional Plane) is an imaginary line that runs horizontally through the abdomen (at the naval) and through the back to divide the body into top and bottom.

Body Cavities:

Abdominopelvic Cavity - A subdivision of the ventral cavity which encases the abdominal cavity and pelvic cavity

Dorsal Cavity - A body cavity which encases the cranial cavity and vertebral canal

Thoracic Cavity - A subdivision of the ventral cavity which is located in the chest and encases the mediastinum, pleural cavity and pericardial cavity

Ventral Cavity- An anterior cavity comprised of the thoracic and abdominopelvic cavities. The abdominopelvic cavity is subdivided into the abdominal cavity and pelvic cavity. The abdominal cavity contains digestive organs, while the pelvic cavity contains the urinary bladder, internal reproductive organs and rectum

Abdominopelvic Quadrants:

Left Upper Quadrant (LUQ) - One of the four quadrants into which the abdominopelvic area is divided. Located in the left upper portion of the abdomen, it includes a view of the stomach, spleen, the left kidney and parts of the duodenum, pancreas, left ureter, small intestine and transverse and descending colon

Left Lower Quadrant (LLQ) - One of the four quadrants into which the abdominopelvic area is divided. Located in the left lower portion of the abdominopelvic area and provides partial views of the small intestine, descending and sigmoid colon, rectum, left ureter and urinary bladder

Right Lower Quadrant (RLQ) - One of the four quadrants into which the abdominopelvic area is divided. Located in the right lower portion of the abdomin-opelvic area, it includes a view of the appendix, cecum and partial views of the ascending colon, small intestine, right ureter, urinary bladder and rectum

Right Upper Quadrant (RUQ) - One of the four quadrants into which the abdominopelvic area is divided. Located in the right upper portion of the abdomen, it provides a view of the gallbladder, most of the liver and partial views of the pancreas, small intestine, ascending and transverse colon

Abdominopelvic Regions

Epigastric Region - One of the six regions into which the abdominopelvic cavity can be divided. It is located in the center of the upper abdomen just below the sternum. It includes partial views of the liver, stomach, pancreas, duodenum and transverse colon

Hypogastric Region - One of the six regions into which the abdominopelvic cavity can be divided. It is located the center of the lower pelvis between the hips. It includes a view of the urinary bladder and rectum, and partial views of the ureters, small intestine and sigmoid colon

Left Hypochondriac Region - One of the six regions into which the abdominopelvic cavity can be divided. It is located in the upper left abdomen, and includes the floating rib cage. It provides a view of the spleen and partial views of the stomach, transverse colon and left kidney

Left Iliac Region - One of the six regions into which the abdominopelvic cavity can be divided. It is located in the left lower pelvic area, and includes the left acetabulum. It provides partial views of the small intestine, descending colon and sigmoid colon

Left Lumbar Region - One of the six regions into which the abdominopelvic cavity can be divided. It is located to the left of the naval, and provides a view of the descending colon and partial views of the left kidney and small intestine

Right Hypochondriac Region - One of the six regions into which the abdominopelvic cavity can be divided. It is located in the upper right abdomen, and includes the floating rib cage. It provides a view of the gallbladder and partial views of the liver, transverse colon and right kidney

Right Iliac Region - One of the six regions into which the abdominopelvic cavity can be divided. It is located in the right lower pelvic area, and includes the right acetabulum. It provides a view of the appendix and cecum and a partial view of the small intestine

Right Lumbar Region - One of the six regions into which the abdominopelvic cavity can be divided. It is located to the right of the naval, and provides a view of the ascending colon and partial views of the small intestine and right kidney

Umbilical Region - One of the six regions into which the abdominopelvic cavity can be divided. It is located directly in the center of the abdominopelvic cavity, and provides a partial view of the duodenum, small intestine, kidneys and ureters

Regions of the Head and Neck

Cephalic - the head. Contains smaller facial and cranial regions

Cervical - the neck.

Cranial - the part of the head containing the brain

Facial - the face

Regions of the Trunk

Abdominal - the region located between the lowest ribs and the hip bones

Abdominopelvic - contains both the abdominal and pelvic regions

Axillary - the armpits

Coxal - the hips

Dorsum - the posterior surface of the thorax

Genital - the external reproductive organs

Gluteal - the buttocks

Inguinal - the groin

Lumbar - the lower back

Pectoral - the chest

Perineal - the small region between the anus and the external reproductive organs

Pelvic - the region enclosed by the pelvic bones

Sacral - the region over the sacrum and between the buttocks

Sternal - the region over the breast bone

Vertebral - the region over the back bone

- Prefix: a¬
  Meaning: Without
  Example: Amenorrhea - without a menstruation cycle

- Prefix: ab- , abs¬
  Meaning: away from
  Example: Abrade - to wear away

- Prefix: ad¬
  Meaning: toward, to
  Example: Addiction - involuntary dependence upon a substance or action

- Prefix: ambi¬
  Meaning: both, around
  Example: Ambidextrous - having ability on both sides

- Prefix: an¬
  Meaning: Without
  Example: Anorexia - without appetite

- Prefix: ana¬
  Meaning: up, toward
  Example: Anaphylactic - exaggerated reaction to an antigen or toxin

- Prefix: ante¬
  Meaning: before
  Example: Antepartum - before labor or childbirth

- Prefix:anti¬
  Meaning: against
  Example: Antidepressant - counteracting depression

- Prefix: apo¬
  Meaning: derived, separate
  Example: apodia - congenital absence of feet

- Prefix: auto(o)¬
  Meaning: self
  Example: autogenous - originating within the body

- Prefix: bi¬
  Meaning: twice, double
  Example: bilobular - having two lobes

- Prefix: brachy¬
  Meaning: short
  Example: brachymelia - disproportionate shortness of limbs

- Prefix: brady¬
  Meaning: Slow
  Example: bradypepsia - slowness of digestion

- Prefix: cata¬
  Meaning: Down
  Example: catabolism - breaking down of chemicals in the body

- Prefix: circum¬
  Meaning: around
  Example: circumcision - cutting around the male genitalia

- Prefix: co-; col-; com-; con-; cor¬
  Meaning: together
  Example: collaboration - to bring together the efforts of two or more people

- Prefix: contra¬
  Meaning: against
  Example: contraceptive - to protect against conception

- Prefix: de¬
  Meaning: away from
  Example: delivery - the passage of fetus and placenta away from the genital canal into the external world

- Prefix: di-; dif-; dir-; dis¬
  Meaning: not, separated
  Example: Dislocation - separation of a joint

- Prefix: dia¬
  Meaning: through
  Example: dialysis - blood filtration through artificial kidney function

- Prefix: dys¬
  Meaning: abnormal, difficult
  Example: Dysuria - difficult urination

- Prefix: ect(o)¬
  Meaning: outside
  Example: ectocyst - outer layer of a hydatid cyst

- Prefix: end(o)¬
  Meaning: within
  Example: endoscopy - examination of the interior with a scope

- Prefix: epi¬
  Meaning: over
  Example: Epidemic - widespread disease over large geographical areas

- Prefix: eu¬
  Meaning: well, good, normal
  Example: eutherapeutic - having excellent curative properties

- Prefix: ex¬
  Meaning: out of, away from
  Example: excretion - to pass out of the body

- Prefix: exo¬
  Meaning: external, on the outside
  Example: Exocrine - a type of gland that secretes onto the surface of the body

- Prefix: extra¬
  Meaning: without, outside of
  Example: extraoral - outside or the oral cavity

- Prefix: hemi¬
  Meaning: half
  Example: Hemiplegia - paralysis on one side of the body

- Prefix: hyper¬
  Meaning: above normal, overly
  Example: Hyperglycemia - high blood sugar

- Prefix: hypo¬
  Meaning: below normal
  Example: Hypoglycemia - low blood sugar

- Prefix: infra¬
  Meaning: positioned beneath
  Example: infrapatellar - beneath the patella

- Prefix: inter¬
  Meaning: between
  Example: internal - beneath the surface

- Prefix: intra¬
  Meaning: within
  Example: intranasal - within the nasal cavity

- Prefix: iso¬
  Meaning: equal, same
  Example: isolate - to separate and set apart from others

- Prefix: mal¬
  Meaning: bad, inadequate
  Example: maladie - a disease or illness

- Prefix: meg(a)- megal(o)¬
  Meaning: large
  Example: Megalocardia - enlarged heart

- Prefix: mes(o) ¬
  Meaning: middle, median
  Example: Mesoderm - the middle layer of skin

- Prefix: meta¬
  Meaning: after
  Example: metatarsal - the foot bone after the tarsal bone

- Prefix: micr(o)¬
  Meaning: small, microscopic
  Example: microscopic - minutely small and invisible to the unaided eye

- Prefix: mon(o)¬
  Meaning: single
  Example: Monolocular - having one cavity or chamber

- Prefix: multi¬
  Meaning: many
  Example: multinodular - having many nodes

- Prefix: olig(o)¬
  Meaning: few, little, scanty
  Example: oligodipsia - abnormal lack of thirst

- Prefix: pan-, pant(o)¬
  Meaning: all, entire
  Example: panacea - cure all remedy

- Prefix: per¬
  Meaning: through, intensely
  Example: percutaneous - passage of substance through the skin

- Prefix: pluri¬
  Meaning: several, more
  Example: pluriresistant - having multiple aspects of resistance

- Prefix: poly¬
  Meaning: many
  Example: polyadentitis - inflammation of many lymph nodes

- Prefix: post¬
  Meaning: after, following
  Example: Posterior - the back surface of the body

- Prefix: pre¬
  Meaning: before
  Example: Prenatal - before birth

- Prefix: pro¬
  Meaning: before, forward
  Example: process - the projection, growth, or the action of moving forward

- Prefix: quadra-, quadri¬
  Meaning: four
  Example: Quadrant - one fourth of a circle

- Prefix: re¬
  Meaning: again, backward
  Example: reaction - to render active again

- Prefix: retro¬
  Meaning: behind, backward
  Example: Retroflexion - bending backwards

- Prefix: semi¬
  Meaning: half
  Example: Semicomatose - a state of half consciousness

- Prefix: sub¬
  Meaning: under, inferior
  Example: Subcutaneous - beneath the skin

- Prefix: super¬
  Meaning: more than, above, superior
  Example: supersonic - greater than the speed of sound

- Prefix: supra¬
  Meaning: above, over
  Example: supraanal - above the anus

- Prefix: syl-, sym-, syn-, sys¬
  Meaning: together
  Example: Symbiosis - mutual interdependence

- Prefix: tachy¬
  Meaning: fast
  Example: Tachycardia -rapid heartbeat

- Prefix: trans¬
  Meaning: across, through
  Example: transplant -to transfer from one part to another

- Prefix: ultra¬
  Meaning: beyond, excessive
  Example: ultrasonic -sound waves at higher frequencies than sound

- Prefix: un¬
  Meaning: not
  Example: unconscious -not conscious

- Prefix: uni¬
  Meaning: one
  Example: union -joining of two parts into one

- Root word: Acanth(o)
  Meaning: Spiny, thorny
  Example: acanthion - the tip of the anterior nasal spine

- Root word: Actin(o)
  Meaning: Light
  Example: Actinotherapy - ultraviolet light therapy used in dermatology

- Root word: Aer(o)
  Meaning: Air, gas
  Example: Aerosol - liquid or particulate matter dispersed in air, gas, or vapor form

- Root word: Alge, algesi, algio, algo
  Meaning: Pain
  Example: Analgesic - a pain reducing agent

- Root word: Amyl(o)
  Meaning: Starch
  Example: Amylolysis - hydrolysis of starch unto soluable products

- Root words: Andro
  Meaning: Masculine
  Example: Androsterone - a steroid metabolite found in male urine

- Root words: Athero
  Meaning: Plaque, fatty substance
  Example: Atheroembolism - cholesterol embolism originating from an atheroma

- Root qord: Bacill(i)
  Meaning: Bacilli, bacteria
  Example: Bacillemia - presence of bacilli in the blood

- Root word: Bacteri(o)
  Meaning: Bacteria
  Example: Bacteriocin - a protien toxin produced and released by bacteria

- Root word: Bar(o)
  Meaning: Weight, pressure
  Example: Bartaxis - reaction of living tissue to changes in pressure

- Root words: Bas(o), basi(o)
  Meaning: Base
  Example: Basoplasm - part of cytoplasm that stains readily with basic dyes

- Root words: Bio¬
  Meaning: Life
  Example: Biopsy - sampling of tissue from living patients

- Root words: Blast(o)
  Meaning: Immature cells
  Example: blastoma - a neoplasm composed of immature cells

- Root words: Cac(o)
  Meaning: Bad, ill
  Example: cacomelia - congenital deformity of one or more limbs

- Root words: Calc(o), calci(o)
  Meaning: Calcium
  Example: Calcipenia - a condition of insufficient calcium

- Root words:Carcin(o)
  Meaning: Cancer
  Example: Carcinogen - cancer-producing substance

- Root words: Chem (o)
  Meaning: Chemical
  Example: Chemotherapy - the treatment of disease by the use of chemicals

- Root words: Chlor (o)
  Meaning: Chlorine, Green
  Example: Chloropenia - a deficiency in chloride

- Root words: Chondrio, Chondro
  Meaning: Cartilage, grainy, gritty
  Example: Chondropathy - ant diese of the cartilage

- Root words: Chore (o)
  Meaning: Dance
  Example: Choreoathetosis - abnormal body movements

- Root word: Chrom, Chromat, Chromo
  Meaning: Color
  Example: Chromatism - abnormal pigmentation

- Root word: Chrono
  Meaning: Time
  Example: Chonopharmicology - the study of the effects of drugs based on the timing of biological events and cycles.

- Root word: Chyl (o)
  Meaning: Chyle, digestive juice
  Example: Chylidrosis - sweating of milky fluid that resembles chyle

- Root word: Chym (o)
  Meaning: Chyme, semifluid produced of chyl and partially digested food
  Example: Chymorrhe - the flow of chyme

- Root word: Cine (o)
  Meaning: Movement
  Example: Cineradiography - the radiography of an organism on motion

- Root word: Coni (o)
  Meaning: Dust
  Example: Coniosis - any disease or morbid condition caused by dust

- Root word: Crin (o)
  Meaning: Secrete
  Example: Crinin - an old term for a substance that stimulates the production of secretion by specific glands

- Root word: Cry (o)
  Meaning: Cold

  Example: Cryospasm - movement of muscles caused by cold

- Root word: Crypt (o)
  Meaning: Hidden, Obscure
  Example: Cryptorchidism - failure of one or both testicals to descend

- Root word: Cyan (o)
  Meaning: Blue
  Example: Cyanosis - a darkblue or purplish color to the skin or mucous membranes

- Root word: Cycl (o)
  Meaning: Circle, Cycle, Cilliary body
  Example: Cyclectomy - excision of a portion of a ciliary body

- Root word: Cyst, Cyst (o)
  Meaning: Bladder, Cyst, Cystic duct
  Example: Cystitis - inflammation of the urinary bladder

- Root word: Cyt (o)
  Meaning: Cell
  Example: Cytocidal - causing the death of cells

- Root word: Dextr (o)
  Meaning: Right, toward right
  Example: Dexter - leaning toward or relating to the right side

- Root word: Dips (o)
  Meaning: Thirsty
  Example: Polydipsia - excessively thirsty

- Root word: Dors (o), dorsi
  Meaning: Back
  Example: Dorsolumbar - the lower back

- Root word: Dynamo
  Meaning: Force, energy
  Example: Dynamogenic - Power produced by muscular and neural activity

- Root word: Echo
  Meaning: Reflected sound
  Example: Echographer - an ultrasonographer

- Root word: Electro (o)
  Meaning: Electricity, electric
  Example: Electrolyte - A compound in body fluid that conducts electricity

- Root word: Eosin (o)
  Meaning: Red, rosy
  Example: Eosiniphobia - A morbid fear of the dawn

- Root word: Ergo
  Meaning: Work
  Example: Ergodynamograph - Used to record the degree of muscle force and the amount of work done by muscle contraction

- Root word: Erythro (o)
  Meaning: Red, redness
  Example: Erythrocatalysis - Phagocytosis of RBC

- Root word: Esthesio
  Meaning: Sedation, perception
  Example: Esthesiology - The study of sensory phenomenon

- Root word: Ethmo
  Meaning: Ethmoid bone
  Example: Ethmoiditis - Inflammation of the ethmoid sinuses

- Root word: Etio
  Meaning: Cause
  Example: Etiology - The study of the cause of diseases and their mode of operation

- Root word: Fibr (o)
  Meaning: Fiber
  Example: Fibroadipose - Relating to or containing both fibrous and fatty structures

- Root word: Fluor (o)
  Meaning: Light, luminous, fluorine
  Example: Fluorocyte - Term used for a reticulocyte that exhibits fluorescence

- Root word: Fungi
  Meaning: Fungus
  Example: Fungitoxic - Poisonous to the growth of fungus

- Root word: Galact (o)
  Meaning: Milk
  Example: Galactocele - Retention of cyst caused by a blocked or narrowing milk duct

- Root word: Gen (o)
  Meaning: Producing, being born
  Example: Genotoxic - A substance that damages DNA and causes in utero mutation or cancer

- Root word: Gero, geront (o)
  Meaning: Old age
  Example: Gerontotherapy - Treatment of disease in the aged

- Root word: Gluco
  Meaning: Glucose
  Example: Glucopenia - low blood sugar

- Root word: Glyco
  Meaning: Sugars
  Example: Glycolipid - A lipid with one or more covalently attached sugar

- Root word: Gonio
  Meaning: Angle
  Example: Gonioscope - A lens designed for the study of the angle of the anterior chamber of the eye

- Root word: Granulo
  Meaning: Granular
  Example: Granuloplastic - forming granules

- Root word: Gyn (o), gyne, gyneco
  Meaning: Women
  Example: Gynecology - The study of genitalia diseases, endocrinology, and reproductive physiology in women

- Root word: Home (o), homo
  Meaning: Same, constant
  Example: Homonuclear - A cell line that retains the original chromosome complement

- Root word: Hydro (o)
  Meaning: Hydrogen, water
  Example: Hydropenia - Reduction or deprivation of water

- Root word: Hypn (o)
  Meaning: Sleep
  Example: Hypnopompic - The occurrence of visions or dreams duringa drowsy state following sleep

- Root word: Iatr (o)
  Meaning: Physician, treatment
  Example: Iatrogenic - The response to medical or surgical treatment, usually when response is unfavorable

- Root word: Ichthy (o)
  Meaning: Dry, scaly, fish
  Example: Ichthyism - Poisoning by eating stale fish

- Root word: Idio
  Meaning: Distinct, unknown
  Example: Idiopathic - Of unknown origin

- Root word: Immun (o)
  Meaning: Safe, immune
  Example: Immunosuppressant - An agent that weakens or suppress the immune system

- Root word: Kal (i)
  Meaning: Potassium
  Example: Hypokalemia - Too little potassium present in the blood

- Root word: Karyo
  Meaning: Nucleus
  Example: Karyoplast - A cell nucleus surrounded by a narrow band of cytoplasm and plasma membrane

- Root word: Ket (o), keton (o)
  Meaning: Ketone, acetone
  Example: Ketoacidosis - Acidosis, usually in diabetics or anorexics, caused by enhanced production of ketone bodies

- Root word: Kin (o), kine
  Meaning: Movement
  Example: Kinometer - An instrument used to measure movement

- Root word: Kinesi (o), kineso
  Meaning: Motion
  Example: Kinesthesia - The sense perception of movement

- Root word: Kyph (o)
  Meaning: Humpback
  Example: Kyphoplasty - Injection of bone cement into a compressed vertebra

- Root word: Lact (o), lacti
  Meaning: Milk
  Example: Lactate - To produce Milk in the mammary glands

- Root word: Latero
  Meaning: Lateral, to one side
  Example: Laterotrusion - The movement of the jaw bone when chewing

- Root word: Lepto
  Meaning: Light, frail, thin
  Example: Leptocephalous - Having an abnormally tall, narrow cranium

- Root word: Leuk (o)
  Meaning: White
  Example: Leukocytosis - A condition of elevated WBC

- Root word: Lip (o)
  Meaning: Fat
  Example: Liposuction - Removal of unwanted fat by use of a suction cannulae

- Root word: Lith (o)
  Meaning: Stone
  Example: Ureterolithiasis - Formation of one or more calculi in one or both ureters

- Root word: Log (o)
  Meaning : Speech, words, thoughts
  Example: Logopathy - Speech disorder

- Root word: Lys (o)
  Meaning: Dissolution
  Example: Lysis - The destruction of RBC, bacteria, ect. by a specific lysin

- Root word: Macr (o)
  Meaning: Large, long
  Example: Macroscopic - Visible to the naked eye

- Root word: Medi (o)
  Meaning: Middle, medial place
  Example: Mediodorsal - Relating to the median and dorsal planes

- Root word: Meg (a), megal (o)
  Meaning: Large, million
  Example: Megalocardia - Enlarged heart

- Root word: Melan (o)
  Meaning: Black, dark
  Example: Melanuria - Excretion of dark colored urine

- Root word: Mes (o)
  Meaning: Middle, median
  Example: Mesocardia - Atypical location of the heart in the central thorax

- Root word: Micr (o)
  Meaning: Small, one-millionth, tiny
  Example: Microscopic - Visible only with the aid of a microscope; of minute size.

- Root word: Mio
  Meaning: Smaller, less
  Example: Miosis - Contraction of the pupil

- Root word: Morph (o)
  Meaning: Structure, shape
  Example: Morphosis - Mode of development of a part

- Root word: Narco
  Meaning: Sleep, numbness
  Example: Narcolepsy -Sleep disorder causing frequent day sleep and interrupted night sleep

- Root word: Necr (o)
  Meaning: Death, dying
  Example: Necrosis -Pathological death of one or more cells, tissue, or organs with irreversiblechanges

- Root word: Noct (i)
  Meaning: Night
  Example: Nocturnal -pertaining to the hours of darkness

- Root word: Norm (o)
  Meaning: Normal
  Example: Normobaric -The barometric pressure equivalent to the pressure at sea level

- Root word: Nucle
  Meaning: Nucleus
  Example: Nucleon -One of the subatomic partials of anomic partials, ex. Proton

- Root word: Nyct (o)
  Meaning: Night
  Example: Nyctophobia -Morbid fear of night time or darkness

- Root word: Oncho, onco
  Meaning: Tumor
  Example: Oncology -The study of neoplastic growths

- Root word: Orth (o)
  Meaning: Straight, normal
  Example: Orthodontics -Dental specialty concerned with the correction of tooth placement

- Root word: Oxy
  Meaning: Sharp, acute, oxygen
  Example: Oxyphonia -Shrill or high pitch of the voice

- Root word: Pachy
  Meaning: Thick
  Example: Pachyblepharon -Thickening of the tarsal boarder of the eyelid

- Root word: Path (o)
  Meaning: Disease
  Example: Pathogen -Disease causing substance

- Root word: Phago
  Meaning: Eating, devouring, swallowing
  Example: Phagocyte -A cell that ingests bacteria and other intruders

- Root word: Pharmaco
  Meaning: Drugs, medicine
  Example: Pharmacology -The study of drugs

- Root word: Phon (o)
  Meaning: Sound, voice, speech
  Example: Phonetics -The science of speech and pronunciation

- Root word: Phot (o)
  Meaning: Light
  Example: Photogen - A microorganism that produced luminescence

- Root word: Physic, physio
  Meaning: Physical, natural
  Example: Physiotherapeutic - Pertaining to physical therapy

- Root word: Physo
  Meaning: Air, gas, growing
  Example: Physocele - Herniated sac distended with gas

- Root word: Phyt (o)
  Meaning: Plant
  Example: Phytodermatitis - Dermatitis caused by skin contacting and reacting to specific plants

- Root word: Plasma, plasmo
  Meaning: Formative, plasma
  Example: Plasmoschisis - The splitting of protoplasm into fragments

- Root Word: Plasma, plasmo
  Meaning: Formative, plasma
  Example: Plasmoschisis - The splitting of protoplasm into fragments

- Root word: Poikilo
  Meaning: Varied, irregular
  Example: Poikiloblast - A nucleated RBC of irregular shape

- Root word: Pseud (o)
  Meaning: False
  Example: Pseudoapraxia - A condition of exaggerated awkwardness in which an individual make wrong use of objects

- Root word: Pyo
  Meaning: Pus
  Example: Pyuria - Pus in the urine

- Root word: Pyreto
  Meaning: Fever
  Example: Pyretogenesis - The origin of a fever

- Root word: Pyro
  Meaning: Fever, fi re, heat
  Example: Pyrolysis - Decomposition of a substance by heat

- Root word: Radio
  Meaning: Radiation, x-ray, radius
  Example: Radiologist - A physician trained in diagnostic / therapeutic use of x-ray and radionuclides

- Root word: Salping (o)
  Meaning: Tube
  Example: Salpingoophorectomy - Removal of the ovary and its uterine tube

- Root word: Schisto
  Meaning: Split
  Example: Schisocelia - Congenital fi ssure of the abdominal wall

- Root word: Schiz (o)
  Meaning: Split, division
  Example: Schizotonia - Division of the distribution of tone in the muscle

- Root word: Scler (o)
  Meaning: Hardness, hardening
  Example: Scleroblastema - The embryonic tissue entering into the formation of bone

- Root word: Scolio
  Meaning; Cooked, bent
  Example: Scoliosis - Condition of abnormal lateral and rotational spine curvature

- Root word: Scoto
  Meaning: Darkness
  Example: Scotopic - Referring to low illumination in which the eye is dark adapted

- Root word: Sidero
  Meaning: Iron
  Example: Siderocyte - An erythrocyte containing granules of free iron

- Root word: Sito
  Meaning: Food, grain
  Example: Sitosterol - A plant-derived chemical similar to cholesterol, commonly found in wheat germ, soy beans, and corn oil.

- Root word: Somat (o)
  Meaning: Body
  Example: Somatalgia - Pain in the body

- Root word: Sono
  Meaning: Sound
  Example: Ultrasonography - containing few or no echoes of sound waves

- Root word: Spasmo
  Meaning: Spasm
  Example: Spasmogen - A substance causing a smooth muscle to contract

- Root word: Sphere (o)
  Meaning: Round, spherical
  Example: Sphereocytosis - The presence of sheric RBCs in the blood

- Root word; Spir (o)
  Meaning: Breath, breathe
  Example: Spiroscope - A device for measuring air capacity in the lungs

- Root word: Squamo
  Meaning: Scale, squamous
  Example: Squamocellular - Relating to or having squamous epithelium

- Root word: Staphyl (o)
  Meaning: Grapelike cluster
  Example:Staphylococcus - Common species that is the cause of a variety of infections

- Root word: Steno
  Meaning: Narrowness
  Example: Stenosis - A narrowing or stricture of any canal or orifice

- Root word: Stere (o)
  Meaning: Three-dimensional
  Example: Stereology - A study of three-dimensional aspects of a cell or microscopic structure

- Root word: Strepto
  Meaning: Twisted chains, streptococci
  Example: Streptococcus - A common organism that causes various infections

- Root word: Styl (o)
  Meaning: Peg-shaped
  Example: Stylomastoid - Relating to the styloid and mastoid processes of the temporal bone

- Root word: Syring (o)
  Meaning:
  Example: Syringe - An instrument used for injecting or withdrawing fluid

- Root word: Tel (o), tele (o)
  Meaning: Distant, end, complete
  Example: Teletherapy - Radiation treatment administered with the source at a distance from the body

- Root word: Terato
  Meaning: Monster (as in malformed fetus)
  Example: Teratogen - An agent that causes a malformed fetus

- Root word: Therm (o)
  Meaning: Heat
  Example: Thermometer - An instrument used to measure temperature

- Root word: Tono
  Meaning: Tension, pressure
  Example: Tonometry - Measurement of tension ex. Blood pressure

- Root word: Top (o)
  Meaning: Place, topical
  Example: Topophobia - A neurotic dread of a particular place

- Root word: Tox (i), toxico, toxo
  Meaning: Poison, toxin
  Example: Toxicoid - Having an action like that of a poison

- Root word: Tropho
  Meaning: Food, nutrition
  Example: Trophodynamics - The dynamics of nutrition or the metabolism (nutritional energy)

- Root word: Vivi
  Meaning: Life
  Example: Vivisection - Any cutting operation on a living animal for purposes of experimentation

- Root word: Xanth (o)
  Meaning: Yellow
  Example: Xanthoma - A yellow nodule or plaque

- Root word: Xeno
  Meaning: Stranger
  Example: Xenograft - A graft transfer from one species to another

- Root word: Xer (o)
  Meaning: Dry
  Example: Xerochilia - Dryness of the lips

- Root word: Xiph (o)
  Meaning: Sword, xiphoid
  Example: Xiphopagus - Conjoined twins united in the region of the xiphoid process

- Root word: Zo (o)
  Meaning: Life
  Example: Zoograft - A graft from an animal to a human

- Root word: Zym (o)
  Meaning: Fermentation, enzyme
  Example: Zygote - Diploid cell resulting from the union of a sperm and a secondary oocyte

- Suffix: -ad
  Meaning: Toward
  Example: Cephalad - toward the head

- Suffix: -algia
  Meaning: Pain
  Example: Cervicalgia - neck pain

- Suffix: -asthenia
  Meaning: Weakness
  Example: Myasthenia - muscle weakness

- Suffix: -blast
  Meaning: Immature, forming
  Example: Cytoblast - immature cell

- Suffix: -cele
  Meaning: Hernia
  Example: Hydrocele - a collection of serous fluid in a sacculated cavity

- Suffix: -cidal, -cide
  Meaning: Destroying, killing
  Example: Cytocide - an agent that is destructive to cells

- Suffix: -clasis
  Meaning: Breaking
  Example: Osteoclasis - intentional breaking of the bone

- Suffix: -clast
  Meaning: Breaking instrument
  Example: Cranioclast - an obsolete instrument used for crushing the head of a demised fetus for extraction

- Suffix: -crine
  Meaning: Secreting
  Example: Apocrine - gland that secretes hormones

- Suffix: -crit
  Meaning: Separate
  Example: Hematocrit - percentage of volume of blood sample that is composed of cells

- Suffix: -cyte
  Meaning: Cell
  Example: Leukocyte - white blood cell

- Suffix: -cytosis
  Meaning: Condition of cells
  Example: Leukocytosis - condition of elevated white blood cells

- Suffix: -derma
  Meaning: Skin
  Example: Leukoderma - an absence of pigment in the skin

- Suffix: -desis
  Meaning: Binding
  Example: Pleurodesis - a fibrous adheasion between two layers of pleura

- Suffix: -dynia
  Meaning: Pain
  Example: Gastrodynia - stomach ache

- Suffix: -ectasia
  Meaning: Expansion, dilation
  Example: Angiectasia - dilation of a lymphatic or blood vessel

- Suffix: -ectomy
  Meaning: Removal of
  Example: Splenectomy - removal of spleen

- Suffix: -edema
  Meaning: Swelling
  Example: Myxedema - hypothyroid charecterized by a hard swelling of subcutaneous tissue

- Suffix: -ema
  Meaning: Condition
  Example: Emphysema - a condition of the lungs involving enlarged air space in connective tissue

- Suffix: -emesis
  Meaning: Vomiting
  Example: Hyperemesis - excessive vomiting

- Suffix: - emia
  Meaning: Blood
  Example: Hypokalemia - abnormal low potassium in the blood

- Suffix: -emic
  Meaning: Relating to blood
  Example: Hyperemic - denoting increased blood flow to a part or organ

- Suffix: -esthesia
  Meaning: Sensation
  Example: Parasthesia - abnormal sensation, such a tingling

- Suffix: -form
  Meaning: In the shape of
  Example: Chloroform - used as an inhalent to produce general anesthesia

- Suffix: -gen
  Meaning: A substance or agent producing, coming to be
  Example: Oxygen - gaseous element essential to plant and animal life

- Suffix: -genesis
  Meaning: Production of
  Example: Osteogenesis - the production of bone

- Suffix: -genic
  Meaning: Producing
  Example: Cytogenic - forming or producing of cells

- Suffix: -globin
  Meaning: Protein
  Example: Hemaglobin - protein of red blood cells

- Suffix: -globulin
  Meaning: Protein
  Example: Gamma-globulin - a protiet in the blood, ie. immunoglobulin

- Suffix: -gram
  Meaning: A recording
  Example: Arthrogram - imaging of a joint by contrast material

- Suffix: -graph
  Meaning: Recording instrument
  Example: Cardiograph - an instrument for graphically recordingmovements of the heart

- Suffix: -graphy
  Meaning: Process of recording
  Example: Angiography - radiography of blood vessles by contrast agent

- Suffix: -iasis
  Meaning: Pathological condition or state
  Example: Cholelithasis - pressence of stone in the gallbladder

- Suffix: -ic
  Meaning: Pertaining to
  Example: Anemic - pertaining to the blood

- Suffix: -ics
  Meaning: Treatment, practice, body of knowledge
  Example - Pediatric - a medical practice concerned with treatment of children

- Suffix: -ism
  Meaning: Condition, disease, doctrine
  Example: Hypothyroidism - the condition of having an abnormally low producing thyroid

- Suffix: -itis
  Meaning: Inflammation
  Example: Dermatitis - an inflammation of the skin

- Suffix: -kinesia; -kinesis
  Meaning: Movement
  Example: Hyperkinesis - excessive muscular movement

- Suffix: -lepsy
  Meaning: Condition of
  Example: Epilepsy - condition with having seizures

- Suffix: -leptic
  Meaning: Having seizures
  Example: Epileptic - person with epilepsy

- Suffix: -logist
  Meaning: One who practices
  Example: Cartiologist - one who practices medicine of the heart

- Suffix: -logy
  Meaning: Study, practice
  Example: Pathology - study of diseases

- Suffix: -lysis
  Meaning: Destruction of
  Example: Paralysis - loss of power of voluntary movement

- Suffix: -lytic
  Meaning: Destroying
  Example: Hemolytic - agent that is destructive to blood cells

- Suffix: -malacia
  Meaning: Softening
  Example: Osteomalacia - gradual softening of bone

- Suffix: -mania
  Meaning: Obsession
  Example: Pyromania - obsessive thoughts regarding fire

- Suffix: -megaly
  Meaning: Enlargement E
  Example: Cardiomegaly - abnormal enlargement of the heart

- Suffix: -meter
  Meaning: Measuring device
  Examle: Thermometer - used for measuring temperature

- Suffix: -metry
  Meaning: Measurement
  Example: Oximetry - device used to measure oxygen saturation

- Suffix: -oid
  Meaning: Like, resembling
  Example: Hemorrhoid - varicose condition of the external hemorrhoidal vein

- Suffix: -oma
  Meaning: Tumor, neoplasm
  Example: Glioma - neoplasm of the brain

- Suffix: -opia; -opsia
  Meaning: Vision
  Example: Diplopia - double vision

- Suffix: -opsy
  Meaning: View of
  Example: Autopsy - examination of a dead body's organs

- Suffix: -osis
  Meaning: Condition, state, process
  Example: Keratosis - any lesion on the skin marked by overgrowths from the horny layer

- Suffix: -ostomy
  Meaning: Opening
  Example: Tracheostomy - surgical opening in the trachea

- Suffix: -oxia
  Meaning: Oxygen
  Example: Hypoxia - abnormally low levels of oxygen prior to anoxia

- Suffix: -para
  Meaning: Bearing
  Example: Primipara - woman who has given birth once

- Suffix: -paresis
  Meaning: Slight paralysis
  Example: Hemiparesis - weakness effecting one side of the body

- Suffix: -parous
  Meaning: Producing, bearing
  Example: Gemmiparous - reproducing by buds

- Suffix: -pathy
  Meaning: Disease
  Example: Cardiopathy - any disease of the heart

- Suffix: -penia
  Meaning: Deficiency
  Example: Thrombocytopenia - condition of low numbers of thrombocytes in the blood

- Suffix: -pepsia
  Meaning: Digestion
  Example: Hyperpepsia - abnormally rapid digestion

- Suffix: -pexy
  Meaning: Fixation, usually done surgically
  Example: Hysteropexy - fixation of a displaced uterus

- Suffix: -phage; -phagia; -phagy
  Meaning: Eating, devouring
  Example: Macrophage - a cell that eats invaders

- Suffix: -phasia
  Meaning: Speaking
  Example: Dyshasia - difficulty in swallowing

- Suffix: -pheresis
  Meaning: Removal
  Example: Leukapheresis - removal of leukocytes from drawn blood

- Suffix: -phil; -philia
  Meaning: Attraction, affinity for
  Example: Hemephilia - permenant tendencey toward bleeding

- Suffix: -phobia
  Meaning: Fear
  Example: Agoraphobia - irrational fear of the open or unfamiliar

- Suffix: -phonia
  Meaning: Sound
  Example: Dysphonia - altered voice production

- Suffix: -phoresis
  Meaning: Carrying
  Example: Diaphoresis - perspiration

- Suffix: -phoria
  Meaning: Feeling, carrying
  Example: Adiphoria - non-response to stimuli

- Suffix: -phrenia
  Meaning: Of the mind
  Example: Hebephrenia - a disorganized type of schizophrenia

- Suffix: -phthisis
  Meaning: Wasting away
  Example: Hemophthisis - anemia

- Suffix: -phylaxis
  Meaning: Protection
  Example: Anaphylaxis - a severe reaction to an agent the body recognizes as an invader

- Suffix: -physis
  Meaning: Growing
  Example: Epiphysis - part of a long bone distinct from and growing out of the shaft

- Suffix: -plakia
  Meaning: Plaque
  Example: melanoplakia - colored patches on the mucous membrane

- Suffix: -plasia
  Meaning: Formation
  Example: Hyperplasia - an increase of the normal number of cells in an organ

- Suffix: -plasm
  Meaning: Formation
  Example: Cytoplasm - a substance of protoplasm in a cell

- Suffix: -plastic
  Meaning: Forming
  Example: Neoplastic - containing a neoplasm or the charecteristics of one

- Suffix: -plasty
  Meaning: Surgical repair
  Example: Dermaplasty - surgical repair of the skin

- Suffix: -plegia
  Meaning: Paralysis
  Example: Paraplegia - paralysis of both lother extremities

- Suffix: -plegic
  Meaning: One who is paralyzed
  Example: Paraplegic - one who has pariplegia

- Suffix: -pnea
  Meaning: Breath
  Example: Dyspnea - difficult or abnormal breathing

- Suffix: -poiesis
  Meaning: Formation
  Example: Thrombopoiesis - formation of thrombocytes

- Suffix: -poietic
  Meaning: Forming
  Example: Erythropoietic - of the formation of red blood cells

- Suffix: -poietin
  Meaning: One that forms
  Example: Erythropoietin - an acid that aids in the formation of red blood cells

- Suffix: -porosis
  Meaning: Lessening in density
  Example: Osteoporosis - lessening if bone density

- Suffix: -ptosis
  Meaning: Falling down, drooping
  Example: Nephroptosis - when the kidney sinks into the pelvis cavity

- Suffix: -rrhage
  Meaning: Discharging heavily
  Example: Hemorhhage - to bleed heavily

- Suffix: -rrhagia
  Meaning: Heavy discharge
  Example: Menorrhagia - Excessive mestrual bleeding

- Suffix: -rrhaphy
  Meaning: Surgical suturing
  Example: Colorrhaphy - suture of the colon

- Suffix: -rrhea
  Meaning: A flowing, a flux
  Example: Rhinorrhea - runny nose

- Suffix: -rrhexis
  Meaning: Rupture
  Example: Angiorrhexis - ruptured blood vessel

- Suffix: -schisis
  Meaning: Splitting internal body cavity
  Example: Spondyloschisis - failure of fusion of the vertebral arch in an embryo

- Suffix: -scope
  Meaning: Instrument (especially one used for observing)
  Example: Laparoscope - a scope used for examining the peritoneal cavity

- Suffix: -scopy
  Meaning; Use of an instrument for observing
  Example: Endoscopy - use of instruments to view an

- Suffix: -somnia
  Meaning: Sleep
  Example: Hypersomnia - excessive day time sleep

- Suffix: -spasm
  Meaning: Contraction
  Example: Myospasm - spasmotic contractions of the muscle

- Suffix: -stalsis
  Meaning: Contraction
  Example: Retrostalsis - backward motion of the intestine

- Suffix: -stasis
  Meaning: Stopping, constant
  Example: Cholestasis - a condition where bile flow from the liver is blocked

- Suffix: -stat
  Meaning: Agent to maintain a state
  Example: Hemostat - an agent that arrests the blow of blood

- Suffix: -static
  Meaning: Maintaining a state
  Example: Orthostatic - relating to an erect posture

- Suffix: -stenosis
  Meaning: Narrowing
  Example: Aortic stenosis - a narrowing of the aortic valve

- Suffix: -stomy
  Meaning: Opening
  Example: Gastrostomy - surgical opening in the stomach (usually for a feeding tube)

- Suffix: -tome
  Meaning: Cutting instrument, segment
  Example: Dermatome - an instrument for making thin slices of the skin

- Suffix: -tomy
  Meaning: Cutting operation
  Example: Craniotomy - surgical operation that removes a portion of the skull to acess the brain

- Suffix: -trophic
  Meaning: Nutritional
  Example: Hypotrophic - progressive degeneration of organs and tissue

- Suffix: -trophy
  Meaning: Nutrition
  Example: Atrophy - a wasting away of the body

- Suffix: -tropia
  Meaning: Turning
  Example: Anatropia - deviation of the axis of one eye upward

- Suffix: -tropic
  Meaning: Turning toward
  Example: Dexiotropic - twisting in a spiral fashion from left to right

- Suffix: -tropy
  Meaning: Condition of turning toward
  Example: Neurotropy - affinity of certain contrasts mediums for nervous tissue

- Suffix: -uria
  Meaning: Urine
  Example: Dysuria - painful or difficult urination

- Suffix: -version
  Meaning: Turning
  Example: Retroversion - a turning backward

Proctor - to - Coder Instructions
To Be Read to Examinees

1. Welcome to the AAPC Certification Coding Exam. My name is **[state your name]** and this is **[state second proctor's name.]** We are the proctors for your examination today.

2. Each of you has been given a copy of the Proctor-To- Coder Instructions along with an exam packet. Your exam packet contains a test grid, marking instructions for grid, gold seals and exam booklet. Please open only your exam packet saving the white adhesive label on the plastic shrink-wrap. Set aside the gold seals, and verify you have the correct type of examination booklet for the exam you are taking (CPC®, CPC-H®, CPC-P®, CIRCC®, CPMA®, or Specialty) and then set it aside with the gold seals (do not break the silver seals on your exam booklet yet.)

   Locate the Important Grid Marking Instruction form. Please read carefully, and using a #2 pencil complete form. Once the form is completed it will be collected prior to beginning the exam. If there are any questions regarding how to fill out the grid correctly please inquire now.

3. Using a #2 pencil, please fill out sections A, B and C of the examination answer grid at this time. For Section B, the Index Number is located on the white adhesive label of your exam packet. Please make sure you are filling in each bubble on your test grid completely, reference the upper right hand corner of the test grid for an example.

4. Now complete Section D of the test grid. Please refer to the back of the exam booklet for the exam type, version and exam number. For assistance with your member ID# refer to the white adhesive label, which is located on the exam plastic.

5. The exam length is 5 hours and 40 minutes. Eating or drinking is permitted during the exam, but make sure examination grids remain dry and clean. Breaks are allowed (as needed) during the exam; however the exam clock **will not stop** when an examinee elects to take a break. Only one examinee may take a break and leave the examination room at a time. Removal of any test material from the exam site is strictly prohibited. Any attempt to remove exam materials will disqualify the examinee for certification and result in automatic failure of the examination.

6. Because this is a timed test, there is no requirement for the examination to be completed in a particular order. It is recommended that you complete all questions that require more time. AAPC does advise that examinees should not leave any questions unanswered. You will be notified when 30 minutes of test time is remaining.

7. Upon completion of your exam, locate your gold seals and put them on the top, right side and bottom of your exam booklet (but **do NOT** seal your test grid in the booklet.) Fill out sections F and G on the answer grid and return your exam booklet, test grid (and E/M Audit Sheets, if applicable) to us before exiting the room. If you finish your exam before the 5 hours and 40 minutes are up, you may leave. When exiting the exam room, please be quiet and courteous of other test takers.

8. Any collaborative or disruptive behavior detected during the examination is cause for immediate action (disqualification, etc.) by the proctors. Electronic devices capable of storing and retrieving text, audio books, etc. may not be brought into the examination room. Please turn off and put away all cell phones and/or pagers. Examination content is confidential, therefore, copying questions and/or discussing the questions with others during or following the examination will disqualify you from certification. Removal of any test material from the exam site is strictly prohibited. Any attempt to remove exam materials will disqualify the examinee for certification and result in automatic failure of the examination. Proctors may not clarify test questions during the examination.

9. If at **ANY TIME** during the exam you are distracted because of the exam environment, you may elect to stop taking the exam. The exam will not be graded, your attempt will not be counted and you will need to contact the AAPC to reschedule your exam at a later date.

10. Exam results are usually released within 5 to 7 business days after AAPC receives the exam package back from the proctor. Results will be accessible in your member area on the AAPC web site (www.aapc.com) and official result documents will be mailed within 2 weeks of their receipt at the national office. **Please do not call AAPC for your test results. Exam results are prohibited from being released over the telephone.** We are now ready to begin the examination, you make break the silver seals and open your test booklet. **Use only a #2 pencil to mark your answers and please correctly bubble in each answer on your test grid.** You have 5 hours and 40 minutes to complete the examination, the current time is **[state the time.]** The exam will end at **[state the time.]**

150 Question Medical Coding Exam

Medical Terminology

1. The suffix –ectomy means:
   a. Cutting into
   b. Surgical removal
   c. A permanent opening
   d. Surgical repair

2. The acronym MMRV stands for:
   a. Measles, Mumps and Rubella vaccine
   b. Measles, Mumps and Rosella vaccine
   c. Measles, Mumps, Rubella and Varicella
   d. Measles, Mumps, Rosella and Varicella

3. MRI stands for:
   a. Microwave Recording Instrument
   b. Medical Recording Instrument
   c. Magnetic Resolution Image
   d. Magnetic Resonance Imaging

4. The term "Salpingo-Oophorectomy" refers to:
   a. The removal of the fallopian tubes and ovaries
   b. The surgical sampling or removal of a fertilized egg
   c. Cutting into the fallopian tubes and ovaries for surgical purposes
   d. Cutting into a fertilized egg for surgical purposes

5. PERRLA stands for:
   a. Pupils Equivalent, Rapid in Response to Light and Accommodation
   b. Pupil Equal, Rapid in Response to Light and Accommodation
   c. Pupil Equivalent, Round, Reactive to Light and Accommodation
   d. Pupils Equal, Round, Reactive to Light and Accommodation

6. Cryopreservation is a means of preserving something through:
   a. Saturation
   b. Heat
   c. Freezing
   d. Chemicals

7. Which of the following describes the removal of fluid from a body cavity?
    a. Arthrocentesis
    b. Amniocentesis
    c. Pericardiocentesis
    d. Paracentesis

8. If a surgeon cuts into a patient's stomach he has performed a:
    a. Gastrectomy
    b. Gastrotomy
    c. Gastrostomy
    d. Gastrorrhaphy

9. The terms Nephro and Renal both refer to the same organ.
    a. True
    b. False

10. In the medical term myopathy, the suffix -pathy means disease. What is diseased?
    a. Mind
    b. Muscle
    c. Eye
    d. Nervous System

Anatomy

11. The Radius is the:
    a. Outer bone located in the forearm
    b. Outer bone located in the lower leg
    c. Inner bone located in the forearm
    d. Inner bone located in the lower leg

12. The spleen belongs to what organ system?
    a. Endocrine
    b. Hemic and Lymphatic
    c. Digestive
    d. Nervous

13. The portion of the femur bone that helps make up the kneecap is considered what?
    a. The posterior portion
    b. The proximal portion
    c. The distal portion
    d. The dorsal portion

14. Which of the following is on the right side of the human body?
    a. Appendix
    b. Sigmoid colon
    c. Descending colon
    d. Rectum

15. The Midsagittal plane refers to what portion of the body?
    a. Top
    b. Middle
    c. Bottom
    d. Back

16. Which of the following is not part of the small intestine?
    a. Duodenum
    b. Ileum
    c. Jejunum
    d. Cecum

17. The cochlea is located in the
    a. Tympanic Cavity
    b. Anterior aqueous chamber of the eye
    c. Inner ear
    d. Middle ear

18. The point of an organ or body part nearest the point of attachments is:
    a. Distal
    b. Proximal
    c. Lateral
    d. Medial

19. One of the six major scapulohumeral muscles:
    a. Temporalis
    b. Trapezius
    c. Teres
    d. Trigone

20. The cardia fundus is:
    a. Part of the heart wall that causes contractions
    b. Where the esophagus joins the stomach
    c. A fungal infection that attacks the heart
    d. Part of the female reproductive system

Coding Concepts

21. CPT codes 22840-22848 are modifier 62 exempt.
    a. True
    b. False

22. An ABN must be signed when?
    a. Once the insurance company has denied payment
    b. Before the service or procedure is provided to the patient
    c. After services are rendered, but before the claim is filed
    d. Once the denied claim has been appealed at the highest level

23. Wound exploration codes include the following service(s):
    a. Exploration and repair
    b. Exploration, including enlargement, removal of foreign bodies, repair
    c. Exploration, including enlargement, repair and necessary grafting
    d. Exploration, including enlargement, debridement, removal of foreign bodies, minor vessel ligation and repair

24. The full description of CPT code 24925 is:
    a. Secondary closure or scar revision
    b. Amputation, secondary closure or scar revision
    c. Amputation, arm through humerus; secondary closure or scar revision
    d. Amputation, arm through humerus; with primary closure, secondary closure or scar revision

25. What does "medical necessity" mean?
    a. Without treatment the patient will suffer permanent disability or death
    b. The service requires medical treatment
    c. The condition of the patient justifies the service provided
    d. The care provided met quality standards

26. Which of the following statements is false?

    a. External Causes of Morbidity Codes are in the range V01- Y99.
    b. You may assign as many external cause codes as necessary.
    c. External cause codes are only used in the initial encounter.
    d. External cause codes can never be a principal diagnosis.

27. Which of the following codes allow the use of modifier 51?

    a. 20975
    b. 93600
    c. 31500
    d. 45392

28. Category III codes are temporary codes for emerging technology, services and procedures. If a category III code exists, it should be used instead of an "unlisted procedure" code in category I (example of an unlisted category I code: 60699).

    a. True
    b. False

29. Which of the following statements is not true regarding Medicare Part A?

    a. It helps cover home health care charges.
    b. It helps cover skilled nursing facility charges.
    c. It helps cover hospice charges.
    d. It helps cover outpatient charges.

30. Which of the following is not one of the three components of HIPAA that is enforced by the office for civil rights?

    a. Protecting the privacy of individually identifiable health information
    b. Setting national standards for the security of electronically protected health information
    c. Protecting identifiable information being used to analyze patient safety events and improve patient safety
    d. Setting national standards regarding the transmission and use of protected health information

ICD-10-CM

31. What is the correct ICD-10-CM code(s) for malignant hypertension with stage 3 kidney disease?
    a. I10, N18.3
    b. I12.9
    c. I10
    d. I12.9, N18.3

32. Lucy was standing on a chair in her apartment kitchen and changing a light bulb when she slipped and fell. She struck the glass stovetop, which shattered. She presents to the ER with a simple laceration to her left forearm that has embedded glass particles.
    a. S51.812A, W18.02XA, W25.XXXA, Y92.030
    b. S51.822A, W18.02XA, W25.XXXA, Y92.030, Y93.E9
    c. S51.812A, Y92.030, W07.XXXA, W25.XXXA
    d. S51.822A, W07.XXXA, W25.XXXA, Y93.E9, Y92.030

33. Jim was at a bonfire when he tripped and fell into the flames, sustaining multiple burns. He arrived at the emergency room via ambulance and was treated for second and third degree burns on his face, second degree burns on his upper arms and forearms, and third degree burns on the fronts of his thighs.
    a. T20.20XA, T20.30XA, T22.259A, T22.219A, T24.319A, T31.42, X03.0XXA
    b. T20.30XA, T24.319A, T22.299A, T31.42, X03.0XXA
    c. T20.09XA, T22.099A, T24.099A, T31.64, X03.0XXA
    d. T20.30XA, T22.299A, T24.319A, T31.64, X03.0XXA

34. A 35-year-old pregnant woman who is in her 38th week with her first child is admitted to the hospital. She experiences a prolonged labor during the first stage and eventually gives birth to a healthy baby boy.
    a. O63.0, O09.519, Z37.0
    b. O80, Z37.0
    c. O80, O63.0, O09.519, Z37.0
    d. O63.0, O09.513, Z37.0

35. Henry was playing baseball and slid into second base, where he collided with another player. He presents to the emergency room complaining of pain in the distal portion of his right middle finger. It is swollen and deformed. The physician orders an x-ray and diagnoses Henry with a displaced tuft fracture. He splints the finger, prescribes narcotics for pain, and instructs Henry to follow up with his orthopedist in two weeks.
    a. S62.632A, Y93.64, W51.XXXA, Y92.320
    b. S62.662A, Y93.64, W03.XXXA, Y92.320
    c. S62.392A, Y93.64, W51.XXXA, Y92.320
    d. S62.632A, Y93.67, W03.XXXA, Y92.320

36. A 60 year old male is admitted for detoxification and rehabilitation. He has continuously abused amphetamines to the point that he cannot voluntarily stop on his own and has become dependent. He also has a long-documented history of alcohol abuse and alcoholism. He experiences high levels of anxiety due to PTSD, causing him to use and abuse substances.
    a. F15.10, F15.20, F10.10, F10.20, F41.1, F43.10
    b. F15.20, F10.20, F41.1, F43.10
    c. F19.20, F10.10, F41.1, F43.10
    d. F15.10, F15.20, F10.10, F10.20, F41.1, F43.10

37. A patient with uncontrolled type II diabetes is experiencing blurred vision and an increase in floaters appearing in her vision. She is diagnosed with diabetic retinopathy.
    a. E08.319
    b. E11.311
    c. E11.319
    d. E11.319,Z79.4

38. Signs and symptoms that are associated routinely with a disease process should not be assigned as additional codes, unless otherwise instructed by classification.
    a. True
    b. False

39. A patient who is known to be HIV positive but who has no documented symptoms would be assigned code.
    a. B20
    b. R75
    c. Z21
    d. B97.35

40. A patient fell asleep on the beach and comes in with blisters on her back. She is diagnosed with second degree solar radiation burns.
    a. L55.1
    b. L56.8
    c. T21.23XA
    d. L58.9

HCPCS

41. A patient has a home health aide come to his home to clean and dress a burn on his lower leg. The aide uses a special absorptive sterile dressing to cover a 50 sq. cm. area. She also covers a 38 sq. cm. area with a self-adhesive sterile gauze pad.
    a. A6204, A6403
    b. A6252, A6403
    c. A6252, A6219
    d. A6204, A6219

42. A 12-year-old arrives in his pediatrician's office after colliding with another player during a soccer game. He is complaining of pain in his right wrist. The physician orders an x-ray and diagnoses him with a hairline fracture of the distal radius. He has a short arm fiberglass cast applied and discharges him with follow up instructions.
    a. Q4009
    b. Q4012
    c. Q4022
    d. Q4010

43. A patient with Hodgkin's disease takes Neosar as part of his chemotherapy regimen. He receives 100 mg once a week through intravenous infusion.
    a. J9100
    b. J7502
    c. J9070
    d. J8999

44. A patient with diabetes is fitted for custom molded shoes. What is the code range for such a fitting?
    a. L3201-L3649
    b. A5500-A5513
    c. K0001-K0902
    d. E0100-E8002

45. A 300 lb. paraplegic needs a special size wheelchair with fixed armrests and elevating leg rests.
    a. E1195
    b. E1222
    c. E1160
    d. E1087

E/M 99201-99499

46. A patient comes into her doctor's office for her weekly blood sugar check. The LPN on staff draws her blood, and the visit takes a total of about five minutes.
    a. 99201
    b. 99212
    c. 99211
    d. 99363

47. A three-year-old child is brought into the ER after swallowing a penny. A detailed history and exam are taken on the child and medical decision making is of moderate complexity. The child is admitted to observation for three hours and is then discharged home.
    a. 99218
    b. 99235
    c. 99218; 99217
    d. 99234

48. A 20-month-old child is admitted to the hospital with pneumonia and acute respiratory distress. The physician spends three minutes intubating the child and spends 90 minutes of critical care time stabilizing the patient.
    a. 99291; 99292-25; 31500; J80; J18.9
    b. 99471-25; 31500; R06.89; J18.9
    c. 99291-25; 99292-25; 31500; R06.89; J18.9
    d. 99471; J80; J18.9

49. At the request of a physician who is delivering for a high-risk pregnancy, Dr. Smith, a pediatrician, is present in the delivery room to assist the infant if needed. After thirty minutes the infant is born, but is not breathing. The delivering physician hands the infant to Dr. Smith who provides chest compressions and resuscitates the infant. The pediatrician then performs the initial evaluation and management and admits the healthy newborn to the nursery. What codes should Dr. Smith submit on a claim?
    a. 99360;99465
    b. 99465; 99460
    c. 99360; 99460
    d. 99360; 99465;99460

50. Mr. Johnson is a 79-year-old established patient who is seen by Dr. Anderson for his annual physical exam. During the examination Dr. Anderson notices a suspicious mole on Mr. Johnson's back. The Doctor completes the annual exam and documents a detailed history and exam and the time discussing the patient's need to quit smoking. Dr. Anderson then turns his attention to the mole and does a complete work up. He documents a comprehensive history and examination and medical decision making of moderate complexity. He also called a local dermatologist and made an appointment for Mr. Johnson to see him the next day for an evaluation and biopsy.
    a. 99387, 99205
    b. 99387, 99215
    c. 99397, 99205
    d. 99397, 99215

51. An E/M is made up of seven components, six of which are used in defining the levels of E/M services. The seven components include History, Exam, Medical Decision Making, Counseling, Coordination of Care, Nature of Presenting Problem and Time. Which six of these seven parts help define the level of the E/M service?
    a. History, Exam, Medical Decision Making, Coordination of Care, Nature of Presenting Problem and Time
    b. History, Exam, Medical Decision Making, Counseling, Nature of Presenting Problem and Time
    c. History, Exam, Medical Decision Making, Counseling, Coordination of Care and Nature of Presenting Problem
    d. History, Exam, Medical Decision Making, Counseling, Coordination of Care and Time

Anesthesia 00100-01999

52. The correct anesthesia code for a ventral hernia repair on a 13-month-old child is
    a. 00830
    b. 00834
    c. 00832
    d. 00820

53. A patient is placed under anesthesia to have an exploratory surgery done on her wrist. The surgeon utilizes a small fiber optic scope and investigates the radius, ulna, and surrounding wrist bones. What should the anesthesiologist code for?
    a. 01829
    b. 01820
    c. 01830
    d. 29840

54. When does anesthesia time begin?
    a. After the induction of anesthesia is complete
    b. During the pre-operative exam prior to entering the OR
    c. When the anesthesiologist begins preparing the patient for the induction of anesthesia
    d. Once the supervising physician signs over the patient's care to the anesthesiologist

55. A five month old is brought into the operating room for open heart surgery. The surgeon performs a repair of a small hole that was found in the lining surrounding the patient's heart. Anesthesia was provided, as well as the assistance of an oxygenator pump.
    a. 00560, 99100
    b. 00561
    c. 00567, 99100
    d. 00561, 99100

56. A 72-year-old male with a history of severe asthma is placed under anesthesia to have a long tendon in his upper arm repaired.
    a. 01712-P4, 99100
    b. 01716-P3
    c. 01714-P3, 99100
    d. 01714-P4

57. Which of the following procedures can be coded separately when performed by an anesthesiologist?
    a. Administration of blood
    b. Monitoring of a central venous line
    c. Capnography
    d. Monitoring of an EKG

58. A female who is 17 weeks pregnant is rushed into the OR due to a ruptured tubal pregnancy. She has a severe hemorrhage and has an emergency laparoscopic tubal ligation.
    a. 00851-P5, 99140
    b. 00880-P4
    c. 01965-P5
    d. 00880-P5, 99140

59. A healthy five-year-old male is placed under anesthesia to have a biopsy taken from his left eardrum.
    a. 00120-P1
    b. 00124-P2
    c. 00170-P2
    d. 00126-P1

60 A 75-year-old healthy male patient sustained a hip dislocation following a fall. He is taken to the OR and plans to be placed under general anesthesia prior to the hip reduction. The anesthesiologist begins preparing the patient at 8:15 am. AT 8:30 am the patient is induced with anesthesia and the anesthesiologist is monitoring the patient's vitals, ECG, pulse ox and capnography. The surgeon begins the reduction at 8:45 am and completes the procedure at 9:15am. The anesthesiologist monitors the patient until 9:30 am when he releases the patient to the nurse for postoperative supervision. At 9:45 am the patient is fully alert and taken to recovery. How many minutes of anesthesia time should the anesthesiologist charge for?
    a. 30 minutes
    b. 45 minutes
    c. 1 hour
    d. 1 hour and 15 minutes

61. An 81-year-old female patient with a history of well-controlled Type 2 diabetes and a mild history of asthma presents to the ER with an injured forearm.
X-rays are taken, and she goes to the operating room for an open reduction with internal fixation for a displaced fracture of the right distal radius. The patient was placed in the supine position on the operating table. The right arm was prepped and draped in the normal, sterile fashion. Prior to surgery, the patient was given 1 g of cefazolin intravenously. A tourniquet was placed on the upper arm and inflated to 250 mmHg. An incision was made along the dorsal aspect of the forearm and subcutaneous tissue was dissected to reveal the fractured radius. A curette was used to remove the splintered ends on each side of the fracture and a K-wire was introduced along the radius to stabilize it. A guide pin was placed down the central axis of the radius. A 20mm hole was drilled and a screw was introduced. The K-wire was removed and the wound was thoroughly irrigated with normal saline. The fascia layer was closed with absorbable sutures and the epidermis was closed with monocryl. The wound was dressed with Vaseline gauze, 4x4, and sterile Sof-Rol. The arm was placed in a long-arm velcro splint and a sling. The tourniquet was deflated; the patient was awakened, placed in her hospital bed and taken to the recovery room in fair condition after a total time of 60 minutes.

Estimated blood loss was 15cc. Sponge and needle counts were correct. Only include the the anesthesia procedure(s) and ICD-10-CM diagnostic codes.

    a. 01830-P2, 99100, S52.501A, E11.9, J45.909
    b. 01830-P3, 99100, S52.501 B, E11.9, J45.909
    c. 01810-P2, 99100, S52.501A, Z86.39, Z87.09
    d. 01820-P3, 99100, S52.501B, Z86.39, Z87.09

Integumentary 10021-19499

62. John was in a fight at a bar and presents to the ER with multiple lacerations. The physician evaluates and determines that John has a 2.5cm gash on his left forearm and a 4cm gash on his right shoulder, which both require layered closure. He also has a simple 3cm laceration on his forehead that requires simple closure. What are the codes for the laceration repairs?
    a. 12032-RT, 12031-LT, 12013-59, S51.822A, S41.021A, S01.81XA
    b. 12032, 12013-59, S51.802A, S41.001A, S01.81XA
    c. 13121, 12052-59, S41.009A, S01.81XA
    d. 12032-RT-LT, 12013-59, S51.802A, S41.001A, S01.81XA

63. A patient presents to her dermatologists office with three suspicious looking lesions. The dermatologist evaluates them and determines that the 1.3 cm lesion on the scalp is benign and the 1.5 cm lesion on the neck is premalignant. A 2.5 cm lesion on the dorsal surface of the patient's hand is also evaluated and is determined to be malignant. The dermatologist chooses to ablate all three lesions using electrosurgery.
    a. 17273, 17003, 17110
    b. 17273, 17000, 17003
    c. 17273, 17000, 17110
    d. 17273, 17003

64. An 18-year-old female presents with a cyst of her left breast and her physician performs a puncture aspiration.
    a. 10160
    b. 10060
    c. 10021
    d. 19000

65. OPERATIVE REPORT

Preoperative Diagnosis: Basal Cell Carcinoma
Postoperative Diagnosis: Basal Cell Carcinoma
Location: Mid Parietal Scalp

Procedure:

Prior to each surgical stage, the surgical site was tested for anesthesia and reanesthetized as needed, after which it was prepped and draped in a sterile fashion.

The clinically apparent tumor was carefully defined and debulked prior to the first stage, determining the extent of the surgical excision. With each stage, a thin layer of tumor-laden tissue was excised with a narrow margin of normal appearing skin, using the Mohs fresh tissue technique. A map was prepared to correspond to the area of skin from which it was excised. The tissue was prepared for the cryostat and sectioned. Each section was coded, cut and stained for microscopic examination. The surgeon examined the entire base and margins of the excised piece of tissue. Areas noted to be positive on the previous stage (if applicable) were removed with the Mohs technique and processed for analysis.

No tumor was identified after the final stage of microscopically controlled surgery. The patient tolerated the procedure well without any complication. After discussion with the patient regarding the various options, the best closure option for each defect was selected for optimal functional and cosmetic results.

Preoperative Size: 1.5 x 2.9 cm
Postoperative Size: 2.7 x 2.9 cm

Closure: Simple Linear Closure, 3.5 cm, scalp

Total # of Mohs Stages: 2

Stage	Sections	Positive
I	6	1
II	2	0

    a. 17311, 17315, 17312, 12002
    b. 17311, 17312, 12002
    c. 17311, 17315, 17312
    d. 17311, 17312

66. A patient with a non-healing burn wound on her right cheek is admitted to the OR for surgery. The physician had the patient prepped with a Betadine scrub and draped in the normal sterile fashion. The cheek was anesthetized with 1% Lydocain with 1:800,000 epinephrine (6 cc), and SeptiCare was applied. A skin graft of the epidermis and a small portion of the dermis were taken with a Goulian Weck blade with a six-thousands-of-an–inch-thick shim on the blade. The 25 sq cm graft was flipped and sewn to the adjacent defect with running 5-0 Vicryl. The wound was then dressed with Xeroform and the patient was taken to recovery.

    a. 14041
    b. 15115
    c. 15120
    d. 15758

67. A child is brought into the emergency department after having the fingers on her right hand closed in a car door. The physician evaluates the patient and diagnoses her with a 3 cm laceration to her second finger and a subungual hematoma to her third finger. The physician then proceeds to cleanse the fingers with iodine scrub and inject both digits with 2 mL of 1% lidocaine with epinephrine. The wound on the second finger was then irrigated with 500 cc of NS and explored for foreign bodies or structural damage. No foreign bodies were found and tendons and vessels were intact. The wound was then reapproximated. Three 5-0 absorbable mattress sutures were used to close the subcutaneous tissue and six 6-0 nylon interrupted sutures were used to close the epidermis. The finger was then wrapped in sterile gauze and placed in an aluminum finger splint. The physician checked that the digital block performed on the third finger was still effective. After ensuring the patient's finger was still numb he then proceeded to take an electronic cautery unit and created a small hole in the nail. Pressing slightly on the nail he evacuated the hematoma. The hole was then irrigated with 500 cc of NS and the finger was wrapped in sterile gauze. The patient tolerated both procedures well without complaint.

    a. 12042-F6, 11740-F7
    b. 64400 (x2), 20103-51, 12042-51, 11740-51,59
    c. 20103, 12042-F6, 11740-F7
    d. 20103, 12042-51, F6, 11740-51, F7

68. The size of an excision of a benign lesion is determined by:
    a. Adding together the lesion diameter and the widest margins necessary to adequately excise the lesion.
    b. Adding together the lesion diameter and the narrowest margins necessary to adequately excise the lesion.
    c. The diameter of the lesion only, excluding any margins excised with it.
    d. The depth of the lesion plus the full diameter of the lesion.

69. A simple, single layered laceration requires extensive cleaning due to being heavily contaminated. The code selected would come from code range 12031-12057.
    a. True
    b. False

70. A skin graft where the donor skin comes from another human (often a cadaver) is known as a/an:
    a. Autograft
    b. Acellulargraft
    c. Allograft
    d. Xenograft

71. A patient is being treated for third degree burns to his left leg and left arm, which cover a total of 18 sq cm. The burns are scrubbed clean, anesthetized and three incisions are made with a #11 scalpel, through the tough leathery tissue that is dead, in order to expose the fatty tissue below and avoid compartment syndrome. The burns are then redressed with sterile gauze.
    a. 97597
    b. 97602
    c. 16035, 16036 x2
    d. 16030, 16035, 16036 x2

Musculoskeleta I 20005-29999

72. Medial and lateral meniscus repair performed arthroscopically
    a. 27447
    b. 29868
    c. 29882
    d. 29883

73. A patient comes to the ER complaining of severe wrist pain after falling on her outstretched hands. The physician evaluates the patient, taking a detailed history and a detailed exam, and then makes decision of moderate complexity. Upon examination, the doctor notes that a small portion of bone is protruding through the skin. After x-rays of the forearm and wrist, the patient is diagnosed with an open distal radius fracture of the right arm. The physician provides an IV morphine drip for pain and reduces the fracture. The doctor uses 5-0 absorbable sutures to close the subcutaneous layer above the fracture and 6-0 nylon interrupted sutures to close the surface. The 2.5 cm wound was dressed with sterile gauze and a Spica fiberglass cast stabilized the wrist. The physician prescribes Percocet for pain and instructs the patient to follow up with an orthopedist in a week.
    a. 99284-25, 25574-RT, S52.501B
    b. 99284-57-25, 25605-54-RT, 12031, S52.501 B
    c. 99284-57, 25574-54, S52.501 B
    d. 99284-25, 25605-RT, 12031, S52.501 B

74. A Scapulopexy is found under what heading
    a. Incision
    b. Excision
    c. Introduction
    d. Repair, Revision and/or Reconstruction

75. A patient with muscle spasms in her back was seen in her physician's office for treatment. The area over the myofascial spasm was prepped with alcohol utilizing sterile technique. After isolating it between two palpating fingertips a 25-gauge 5" needle was placed in the center of the myofascial spasms and a negative aspiration was performed. Then 4 cc of Marcaine 0.5% was injected into three points in the muscle. The patient tolerated the procedure well with-out any apparent difficulties or complications. The patient reported feeling full relief by the time the block had set.
    a. 64400
    b. 20552
    c. 64520
    d. 20553

76. **OPERATIVE NOTE**
PREOPERATIVE DIAGNOSIS: myelopathy secondary to very large disc herniations at C4-C5 and C5-C6.

POSTOPERATIVE DIAGNOSIS: myelopathy secondary to very large disc herniations at C4-C5 and C5-C6.

PROCEDURE PERFORMED:
1.   Anterior discectomy, C5-C6.
2.   Arthrodesis, C5-C6.
3.   Partial corpectomy, C5.
4.   Machine bone allograft, C5-C6.
5.   Placement of anterior plate with a Zephyr C6.

ANESTHESIA: General.
ESTIMATED BLOOD LOSS: 60 mL.
COMPLICATIONS: None.

INDICATIONS: This is a patient who presents with progressive weakness in the left upper extremity as well as imbalance. He has a very large disc herniation that came behind the body at C5 as well and as well as a large disc herniation at C5-C6. Risks and benefits of the surgery including bleeding, infection, neurologic deficit, nonunion, progressive spondylosis, and lack of improvement were all discussed. He understood and wished to proceed.

DESCRIPTION OF PROCEDURE: The patient was brought to the operating room and placed in the supine position. Preoperative antibiotics were given. The patient was placed in the supine position with all pressure points noted and well padded. The patient was prepped and draped in standard fashion. An incision was made approximately above the level of the cricoid. Blunt dissection was used to expose the anterior portion of the spine with carotid moved laterally and trachea and esophagus moved medially. I then placed needle into the disc spaces and was found to be at C5-C6. Distracting pins were placed in the body of C6. The disc was then completely removed at C5-C6. There was very significant compression of the cord. This was carefully removed to avoid any type of pressure on the cord. This was very severe and multiple free fragments noted. This was taken down to the level of ligamentum. Both foramens were then also opened. Part of the body of C5 was taken down to assure that all fragments were removed and that there was no additional constriction. The nerve root was then widely decompressed. Machine bone allograft was placed into C5-C6 and then a Zephyr plate was placed in the body C6 with a metal pin placed into the body at C5. Excellent purchase was obtained. Fluoroscopy showed good placement and meticulous hemostasis was obtained. Fascia was closed with 3-0 Vicryl, subcuticular 3-0 Dermabond for skin. The patient tolerated the procedure well and went to recovery in good condition.
    a. 22554, 63081, 63082, 20931, 22845
    b. 22551, 63081, 20931, 22840
    c. 22551, 63081, 63082, 20931, 22845
    d. 22554, 63081, 20931, 22840

77. A general surgeon and a neurosurgeon are performing an osteotomy on the L4 vertebral segment. The general surgeon establishes the opening using an anterior approach. While the neurosurgeon performs the osteotomy, the general surgeon performs a discectomy. After completion, the general surgeon closes the patient up.
    a. General: 22224-59 Neurosurgeon: 22224-54
    b. General: 22224-62 Neurosurgeon: 22224-62
    c. General: 22224-66 Neurosurgeon: 22224-66
    d. General: 22224 Neurosurgeon: 22224-80

78. A patient comes into his physician's office with a prior diagnosis of a Colles type distal radius fracture. He complains that the cast he currently has is too tight and is causing numbness in his fingers. The physician removes the cast to ensure that the patient's circulation is intact. He then reapplies a short arm fiberglass cast and checks the patient's neurovascular status several times during the procedure. The patient is given instructions to follow-up with his orthopedist within seven days.
    a. 25600-77
    b. 25600-52
    c. 29705, 29075
    d. 29075

79. A patient is brought into the OR for a diagnostic arthroscopy of the shoulder. The patient has been complaining of pain since his surgery 4 months ago. The surgeon explores the shoulder and discovers a metal clamp, which had been left in from the prior surgery. The surgeon removed the clamp and closed the patient up.
    a. 29805, 23333
    b. 29805, 29819
    c. 29819-78
    d. 29819

80. A 59-year-old female was brought to the operating room and placed on the surgical table in a supine position. Following anesthesia, the surgical site was prepped and draped in the normal sterile fashion. Attention was then directed to the right foot where, utilizing a #15 blade, a 6 cm. linear incision was made over the 1st metatarsal head, taking care to identify and retract all vital structures. The incision was medial to and parallel to the extensor hallucis longus tendon. The incision was deepened through subcutaneous underscored, retracted medially and laterally - thus exposing the capsular structures below, which were incised in a linear longitudinal manner, approximately the length of the skin incision. The capsular structures were sharply underscored off the underlying osseous attachments, retracted medially and laterally. Utilizing an osteotome and mallet the medial eminence of the metatarsal bone was removed and the head was remodeled with the Liston bone forceps and the bell rasp. The surgical site was then flushed with saline. The base of the proximal phalanx of the great toe was osteotomized approximately 1 cm distal to the base and excised to toto from the surgical site. There was no hemi implant used and Kirschner wire was used to hold the joint in place. Superficial closure was accomplished using Vicryl 5-0 in a running subcuticular fashion. Site was dressed with a light compressive dressing. The tourniquet was released. Excellent capillary refill to all the digits was observed without excessive bleeding noted.
    a. 28290
    b. 28292
    c. 28294
    d. 28298

Respiratory, Cardiovascular, Hemic and Lymphatic, Mediastinum
and Diaphragm 30000-39599

81. **Operative Note**

   PREOPERATIVE DIAGNOSIS: Angina and coronary artery disease.
   POSTOPERATIVE DIAGNOSIS: Angina and coronary artery disease.

   PROCEDURE DETAILS: The patient was brought to the operating room and placed in the
   supine position upon the table. After adequate general anesthesia, the patient was prepped
   with Betadine soap and solution in the usual sterile manner. Elbows were protected to avoid
   ulnar neuropathy and phrenic nerve protectors were used to protect the phrenic nerve. All
   were removed at the end of the case.

   A midline sternal skin incision was made and carried down through the sternum, which was
   divided with the saw. Pericardial and thymus fat pad was divided. The left internal mammary artery was harvested and spatulated for anastomosis. Heparin was given.

   The Femoropopliteal vein was resected from the thigh, side branches secured using 4-0 silk
   and Hemoclips. The thigh was closed multilayer Vicryl and Dexon technique. A Pulsavac
   wash was done and a drain was placed.

   The left internal mammary artery is sewn to the left anterior descending using 7-0 running
   Prolene technique with the Medtronic off-pump retractors. After this was done, the patient
   was fully heparinized, cannulated with a 6.5 atrial cannula and a 2-stage venous catheter
   and begun on cardiopulmonary bypass and maintained normothermia. Medtronic retractors
   used to expose the circumflex. Prior to going on pump, we stapled the vein graft in place to
   the aorta.

   Then, on pump, we did the distal anastomosis with a 7-0 running Prolene technique. The
   right side graft was brought to the posterior descending artery using running 7-0 Prolene
   technique. Deairing procedure was carried out. The bulldog clamps were removed. The
   patient maintained good normal sinus rhythm with good mean perfusion. The patient was
   weaned from cardiopulmonary bypass. The arterial and venous lines were removed and
   doubly secured. Protamine was delivered. Meticulous hemostasis was present. Platelets
   were given for coagulopathy. Chest tube was placed and meticulous hemostasis was present. The anatomy and the flow in the grafts was excellent. Closure was begun.

   The sternum was closed with wire, followed by linea alba and pectus fascia closure with
   running 6-0 Vicryl sutures in double-layer technique. The skin was closed with subcuticular
   4-0 Dexon suture technique. The patient tolerated the procedure well and was transferred
   to the intensive care unit in stable condition.
   a. 35600, 35572, 33533, 33517, 32551, 36825, 33926
   b. 33533, 33517, 35572
   c. 33510, 33533, 35572, 32551, 36821
   d. 33510, 33533, 33572

82. A 50-year-old gentleman with severe respiratory failure is mechanically ventilated and is currently requiring multiple intravenous drips. With the patient in his Intensive Care Unit bed, mechanically ventilated in the Trendelenburg position, the right neck was prepped and draped with Betadine in a sterile fashion. A single needle stick aspiration of the right subclavian vein was accomplished without difficulty and the guide wire was advanced and a dilator was advanced over the wire. The triple lumen catheter was cannulated over the wire and the wire was then removed. No PVCs were encountered during the procedure. All three ports to the catheter were aspirated and flushed blood easily and they were all flushed with normal saline. The catheter was anchored to the chest wall with butterfly phalange using 3-0 silk suture. Betadine ointment and a sterile OpSite dressing were applied. Stat upright chest x-ray was obtained at the completion of the procedure to ensure proper placement of the tip in the subclavian vein.
    a. 36557
    b. 36555
    c. 36558
    d. 36556

83. A patient with chronic emphysema has surgery to remove both lobes of the left lung.
    a. 32440
    b. 32482
    c. 32663x2
    d. 32310

84. A thoracic surgeon makes an incision under the sternal notch at the base of the throat, introduces the scope into the mediastinal space and takes two biopsies of the mediastinal mass. He then retracts the scope and closes the small incision.
    a. 39401
    b. 32606
    c. 39000
    d. 32405

85. A patient has endoscopic surgery performed to remove his anterior and posterior ethmoid sinuses. The surgeon dialated the maxillary sinus with a balloon using a transnasal approach, explored the frontal sinuses, removed two polyps from the maxillary sinus and then performed the tissue removal.
    a. 31255, 31295, 31237
    b. 31201, 31295, 31237
    c. 31255, 31267
    d. 31255, 31295, 31267

86. **Operative Note**

Approach: Left cephalic vein.

Leads Implanted: Medtronic model 5076-45 in the right atrium, serial number PJN983322V. Medtronic 5076-52 in the right ventricle, serial number PJN961008V.

Device Implanted: Pacemaker, Dual Chamber, Medtronic EnRhythm, model P1501VR, serial number PNP422256H.

Lead Performance: Atrial threshold less than 1.3 volts at 0.5 milliseconds. P wave 3.3 millivolts. Impedance 572 ohms. Right ventricle threshold 0.9 volts at 0.5 milliseconds. R wave 10.3. Impedance 855.

Procedure: The patient was brought to the electrophysiology laboratory in a fasting state and intravenous sedation was provided as needed with Versed and fentanyl. The left neck and chest were prepped and draped in the usual manner and the skin and subcutaneous tissues below the left clavicle were infiltrated with 1% lidocaine for local anesthesia. A 2-1/2-inch incision was made below the left clavicle and electrocautery was used for hemostasis. Dissection was carried out to the level of the pectoralis fascia and extended caudally to create a pocket for the pulse generator. The deltopectoral groove was explored and a medium-sized cephalic vein was identified. The distal end of the vein was ligated and a venotomy was performed. Two guide wires were advanced to the superior vena cava and peel-away introducer sheaths were used to insert the two pacing leads. The venous pressures were elevated and there was a fair amount of back-bleeding from the vein, so a 3-0 Monocryl figure-of-eight stitch was placed around the tissue surrounding the vein for hemostasis. The right ventricular lead was placed in the high RV septum and the right atrial lead was placed in the right atrial appendage. The leads were tested with a pacing systems analyzer and the results are noted above. The leads were then anchored in place with #0-silk around their suture sleeve and connected to the pulse generator. The pacemaker was noted to function appropriately. The pocket was then irrigated with antibiotic solution and the pacemaker system was placed in the pocket. The incision was closed with two layers of 3-0 Monocryl and a subcuticular closure of 4-0 Monocryl. The incision was dressed with Steri-Strips and a sterile bandage and the patient was returned to her room in good condition.

    a. 33240, 33225, 33202
    b. 33208, 33225, 33202
    c. 33213, 33217
    d. 33208

87. If a surgeon is performing a surgical sinus endoscopy to control a nasal hemorrhage and chooses to perform a necessary sinusotomy while he's there, he can bill for each individual service.
    a. True
    b. False

88. A cardiologist manipulates a catheter through the patient's atrial system, starting in the femoral artery and manipulating to the third order, using intra-vascular ultrasound. The cardiologist performs radiological supervision and interpretation.
    a. 36217, 37252
    b. 36217, 37252, 37253
    c. 36247, 37252, 37253 X2
    d. 36247, 37252, 37253

89. An indirect laryngoscopy, as described in code 31505, utilizes a mirror in which the physician can view the reflection of the larynx. A direct larngos-copy, as described by code 31515, utilizes a scope in which the physician peers through and views the larynx.
    a. True
    b. False

90. A patient was taken into the operating room. After induction of appropriate anesthesia, her left chest, neck, axilla and arm were prepped with Betadine solution and draped in a sterile fashion. An incision was made at the hairline and carried down by sharp dissection through the clavipecto-ral fascia. The lymph node was palpitated in the armpit and grasped with a figure-of-eight 2-0 silk suture and by sharp dissection, was carried to hemo-clip all attached structures. The lymph node was excised in its entirety. The wound was irrigated. The lymph node was sent to pathology. The wound was then closed. Hemostasis was assured and the patient was taken to recovery room in stable condition.
    a. 38308
    b. 38500
    c. 38510
    d. 38525

Digestive 40490-49999

91. The patient was scheduled for an esophagogastroduodenoscopy. Upon arrival he was placed under conscious sedation and instructed to swallow a small flexible camera. The camera was then manipulated into the esophagus, and through the entire length of the esophagus. The esophagus appeared to be slightly inflamed, but there was no sign of erosion or flame hemorrhage. A small 2cm tissue sample was taken to look for gastroesophageal reflux disease. There was no stricture or Barrett mucosa. The bony and the antrum of the stomach were normal without any acute peptic lesions. Retroflexion of the tip of the endoscope in the body of the stomach revealed an abnormal cardia. There were no acute lesions and no evidence of ulcer, tumor, or polyp. The pylorus was easily entered, and the first, second, and third portions of the duodenum were normal.

    a. 43202
    b. 43234
    c. 43235
    d. 43239

92. After informed consent was obtained, the patient was placed in the left lateral decubitus position and sedated. The Olympus video colonoscope was inserted through the anus and was advanced in retrograde fashion through the sigmoid colon, descending colon and to the splenic flexure. There was a large amount of stool at the flexure, which appeared to be impacted. The physician decided not to advance to the cecum due to the impaction and the scope was pulled back into the descending colon and then slowly withdrawn. The mucosa was examined in detail along the way and was entirely normal. Upon reaching the rectum, retroflex examination of the rectum was normal. The scope was then straightened out, the air removed and the scope withdrawn. The patient tolerated the procedure well.

    a. 45330-53
    b. 45330
    c. 45378-53
    d. 45378

93. Operative Note

The 45-year-old male patient was taken to the operative suite, placed on the table in the supine position and given a spinal anesthetic. The right inguinal region was shaved, prepped and draped in a routine sterile fashion. The patient received 1 gm of Ancef IV push. A transverse incision was made in the intraabdominal crease and carried through the skin and subcutaneous tissue. The external oblique fascia was exposed and incised down to, and through, the external inguinal ring. The spermatic cord and hernia sac were dissected bluntly off the undersurface of the external oblique fascia exposing the at-tenuated floor of the inguinal canal. The cord was surrounded with a Penrose drain. The sac was separated from the cord structures. The floor of the inguinal canal, which consisted of attenuated transversalis fascia, was imbricated upon itself with a running locked suture of 2-0 Prolene. Marlex patch 1 x 4 in dimension was trimmed to an appropriate shape with a defect to accommodate the cord. It was placed around the cord and sutured to itself with 2-0 Prolene. The patch was then sutured medially to the pubic tubercle, inferiorly to Cooper's ligament and inguinal ligaments, and superiorly to conjoined tendon using 2-0 Prolene. The area was irrigated with saline solution, and 0.5% Marcaine with epinephrine was injected to provide prolonged postoperative pain relief. The cord was returned to its position. External oblique fascia was closed with a running 2-0 PDS, subcu with 2-0 Vicryl, and skin with running subdermal 4-0 Vicryl and Steri-Strips. Sponge and needle counts were correct. Sterile dressing was applied.

     a. 49505
     b. 49505, 54520
     c. 49505, 49568
     d. 49505, 54520, 49568

94. The vestibule is part of the oral cavity outside the dentoalveolar structures and includes the mucosal and submucosal tissue of the lips and cheeks.

     a. True
     b. False

95. Which of the following organs is not part of the alimentary canal?

     a. Gallbladder
     b. Duodenum
     c. Jejunum
     d. Tounge

96. A 13-year-old child has his tonsils and adenoids removed due acute tonsillitis and chronic tonsillitis and adenoiditis.

     a. 42826, 42831, J36, J35.0
     b. 42826, 42836, J03.90, J35.03
     c. 42821, J03.90, J35.03
     d. 42821-50, J03.90, J35.0

97. **Operative Note**

Preoperative Diagnosis: Protein-calorie malnutrition
Postoperative Diagnosis: Protein-calorie malnutrition.
Anesthesia: Conscious sedation per Anesthesia.
Complications: None
EGD: Dr. Brown
PEG Placement: Dr. Smith

History: The patient is a 73-year-old male who was admitted to the hospital with some mentation changes. He was unable to sustain enough caloric intake and had markedly decreased albumin stores. After discussion with the patient and his son they agreed to place a PEG tube for nutritional supplementation.

Procedure: After informed consent was obtained the patient was brought to the endoscopy suite. He was placed in the supine position and was given IV sedation by the Anesthesia Department. Dr. Brown, who has dictated his finding separately, performed an EGD from above. The stomach was transilluminated and an optimal position for the PEG tube was identified using the single poke method. The skin was infiltrated with local and the needle and sheath were inserted through the abdomen into the stomach under direct visualization. The needle was removed and a guidewire was inserted through the sheath. Dr. Brown grasped the guidewire with a snare from above. It was removed completely and the Ponsky PEG tube was secured to the guidewire. The guidewire and PEG tube were then pulled through the mouth and esophagus and snug to the abdominal wall. There was no evidence of bleeding. Photos were taken. The Bolster was placed on the PEG site. Dr. Brown will do a complete dictation for the EGD separately. The patient tolerated the procedure well and was transferred to recovery room in stable condition. He will be started on tube feedings in 6 hours with aspiration and dietary precautions to determine his nutritional goal.

What code(s) should Dr. Smith charge?
    a. 43246-62
    b. 49440
    c. 43752
    d. 43653

98. An 18-year-old female was found with a suicide note and an empty bottle of Tylenol. She was rushed into the emergency department where she had a large-bore gastric lavage tube inserted into her stomach and the contents were evacuated.
    a. 43756
    b. 43752
    c. 43753
    d. 43754

99. All endoscopies performed on the digestive system (such as an esophago-scopy, a colonoscopy, a sigmoidoscopy, etc.) do not allow moderate seda-tion to be coded additionally because it is bundled into the code?
    a. True
    b. False

100. **Operative Note**
     History of Present Illness: Ms. Moore is status post lap band placement, the band was placed just over a year ago and she is here for a lap band adjustment. She has a history of problems previously with her adjustments. She has been under a lot of stress recently due to a car accident she was in a couple of weeks ago. Since the accident she has been experiencing problems of "not feeling full". She states that she is not really hungry but she does not feel full either. She also states that when she is hungry at night she is having difficulty waiting until the morning to eat. She also men-tioned that she had a candy bar and that seemed to make her feel better.

     Physical Examination: On exam, her temperature is 98, pulse 76, weight 197.7 pounds, blood pressure 102/72, BMI is 38.5, she has lost 3.8 pounds since her last visit. She was alert and oriented in no apparent distress.

     Procedure: I was able to access her port. She does have an AP standard low profile. I aspirated 6 mL, I did add 1 mL, so she has got approximately 7 mL in her restrictive device, and she did tolerate water post procedure.

     Assessment: The patient's status post lap band adjustments; doing well, has a total of 7 mL within her lap band, tolerated water pos procedure. She will come back in two weeks for another adjustment as needed.
     a. 43771
     b. 43886
     c. 43842
     d. 43848

Urinary, Male Genital, and Female Genital Systems,
and Maternity Care and Delivery 50010 – 59899

101. A patient was brought to the OR and sedated. She was then placed in the supine position on a water filled cushion. The C-Arm image intensifier was positioned in the correct anatomical location above the left renal and a total of 2500 high energy shock waves were applied from the outside of the body. Energy levels were slowly started and O2 increased up to 7. Gradual-ly the 2.5 cm stone was broken into smaller pieces as the number of shocks went up. The shocks were started at 60 per minute and slowly increased up to 90 per minute. The patient's heart rate and blood pressure were stable throughout the entire procedure. She was transported to recovery in good condition.
      a. 50081, 74425
      b. 50130, 76770
      c. 50060
      d. 50590

102. A patient recently underwent a total hysterectomy due to ovarian cancer, which has metastasized. She is now having cylinder rods placed for clini-cal brachytherapy treatment. Treatment will consist of high dose rate (HDR) brachytherapy once correct placement of the rods has been confirmed.
      a. 57155
      a. 57156
      b. 57155-58
      c. 57156-58

103. The patient was brought to the suite, where after oral sedation, the scrotum was prepped and draped. 1% lidocaine was used for local anesthesia. The vas was identified, skin was incised, and no scalpel instruments were used to dissect out the vas. A segment about 3 cm in length was dissected out. It was clipped proximally and distally, and then the ends were cauterized after excising the segment. Minimal bleeding was encountered and the scrotal skin was closed with 3-0 chromic. The identical procedure was performed on the contralateral side. The patient tolerated the procedure well. He was discharged from the surgical center in good condition with Tylenol with Co-deine for pain.
      a. 55450
      b. 55400
      c. 55400-50
      d. 55250

104. Operative Note

Epidural anesthesia was administered in the holding area, after which the patient was transferred into the operating room. General endotracheal anesthesia was administered, after which the patient was positioned in the flank standard position. A left flank incision was made over the area of the twelfth rib. The subcutaneous space was opened by using the Bovie. The ribs were palpated clearly and the fascia overlying the intercostal space between the eleventh and twelfth rib was opened by using the Bovie. The fascial layer covering of the intercostal space was opened completely until the retroperitoneum was entered. Once the retroperitoneum had been entered, the incision was extended until the peritoneal envelope could be identified. The peritoneum was swept medially. The Finochietto retractor was then placed for exposure. The kidney was readily identified and was mobilized from outside Gerota's fascia. The ureter was dissected out easily and was separated with a vessel loop. The superior aspect of the kidney was mobilized from the superior attachment. The pedicle of the left kidney was completely dissected revealing the vein and the artery. The artery was a single artery and was dissected easily by using a right¬angle clamp. A vessel loop was placed around the renal artery. The tumor could be easily palpated in the lateral lower pole to mid pole of the left kidney. The Gerota's fascia overlying that portion of the kidney was opened in the area circumferential to the tumor. Once the renal capsule had been identified, the capsule was scored using a Bovie about 0.5 cm lateral to the border of the tumor. Bulldog clamp was then placed on the renal artery. The tumor was then bluntly dissected off of the kidney with a thin rim of a normal renal cortex. This was performed by using the blunted end of the scalpel. The tumor was removed easily. The argon beam coagulation device was then utilized to coagulate the base of the resection. The visible larger bleeding vessels were oversewn by using 4-0 Vicryl suture. The edges of the kidney were then reapproximated by using 2-0 Vicryl suture with pledgets at the ends of the sutures to prevent the sutures from pulling through. Two horizontal mattress sutures were placed and were tied down. The Gerota's fascia was then also closed by using 2-0 Vicryl suture. The area of the kidney at the base was covered with Surgicel prior to tying the sutures. The bulldog clamp was removed and perfect hemostasis was evident. There was no evidence of violation into the calyceal system. A 19-French Blake drain was placed in the inferior aspect of the kidney exiting the left flank inferior to the incision. The drain was anchored by using silk sutures. The flank fas-cial layers were closed in three separate layers in the more medial aspect. The lateral posterior aspect was closed in two separate layers using Vicryl sutures. The skin was finally reapproximated by using metallic clips. The patient tolerated the procedure well.

    a. 50545
    b. 50240
    c. 50220
    d. 50290

105. A 26 year old patient who is Gravida 2 Para 1 presents to the ER in her 36th week of pregnancy with twin gestations who are monochorionic and monoamniotic. She is in active labor, 6 cm dilated, and her water is intact. Her OBGYN, who provided 12 antepartum visits, admitted her to labor & delivery. Although the patient had a previous cesarean during her first pregnancy the physician allowed her to attempt a vaginal birth. After pushing for three hours the patient was exhausted and taken to the OR for a cesarean delivery with a transverse incision. Two healthy newborns were born 15 minutes later. During the hospital stay and afterward the same physician provided the postpartum care to the mother.
    a. 59426, 59622, 59620, O75.81, O30.013, O60.14X2, Z38.4
    b. 59618, 59620-51, O75.81, O30.013, O60.14XO, O66.41, O82, Z37.2,Z3A.36
    c. 59618, 59618-51, O30.013, O66.41, O82, Z37.2, Z3A.36
    d. 59618-22, O82, O60.14X2, O030.013, Z38.4

106. When reporting delivery only services the discharge should be reported by using an E/M.
    a. True
    b. False

107. A 74-year-old male with a weak urinary stream had his PSA tested. Results read 12.5 and he was scheduled for a biopsy to determine whether he had a malignancy or BPH. He arrived for surgery and was placed in the left lateral decubitus position and sedated. The surgeon used ultrasonic guidance to percutaneously retrieve 3 biopsies, using the transperineal approach. The biopsies were examined and the patient was diagnosed with secondary prostate cancer with the primary site unknown. He was directed to schedule a PET scan and discharged in good condition.
    a. 55875, 76965
    b. 55706, 76942
    c. 55700, 76942
    d. 55705, 76942

108. **Procedure:** Hydrocelectomy

     A scrotal incision was made and further extended with electrocautery. Once the hydrocele sac was reached we then opened and delivered the testis which drained clear fluid. There was moderate amount of scarring on the testis itself from the tunica vaginalis. The hydrocele sac was completely removed. A drain was then placed in the base of the scrotum and then the testis was placed back into the scrotum in the proper orientation. The same procedure was performed on the left. The skin was then sutured with a running interlocking suture of 3-0 Vicryl and the drains were sutured to place with 3-0 Vicryl. Bacitracin dressing, ABD dressing, and jock strap were placed. The patient was in stable condition upon transfer to recovery.
     a. 55041
     b. 54861
     c. 55000-50
     d. 55060

109. A urologist performs a cystometrogram with intra-abdominal voiding pressure studies in a hospital using calibrated electronic equipment that is provided for his use. He interprets the study and diagnosis the patient with neurogenic bladder.
     a. 51726, 51797
     b. 51729-26, 51797-26
     c. 51726-26, 51797-26
     d. 51729, 51797

110. Transvaginal sonographically controlled retrieval of a 26-year-old female's eggs by piercing the ovarian follicle with a very fine needle.
     a. 58976, 76948
     b. 58672
     c. 58970, 76948
     d. 58940, 76948

Endocrine, Nervous, Ocular, and Auditory Systems 60000 – 69990

111. The hammer, anvil and stirrup are the English terms for the three auditory ossicles, whose Latin names are:
     a. Stapes, Utricle, and cochlea
     b. Malleus, incus, and stapes
     c. Utricle, incus, and vestibular nerve
     d. Malleus, stapes, Utricle

112. **Operative Note**

     Pre-operative Diagnosis: Increased intracranial pressure and cerebral edema due to severe brain injury.

     Post operative Diagnosis: Increased intracranial pressure and cerebral edema due to severe brain injury.

     Procedure: Scalp was clipped. Patient was prepped with ChloraPrep and Betadine. Incisions are infiltrated with 1% Xylocaine with epinephrine 1:200000. Patient did receive antibiotics post procedure and was draped in a sterile manner. The incision made just to the right of the right mid-pupillary line 10 cm behind the nasion. A self-retaining retractor was placed. A hole was then drilled with the cranial twist drill and the dura was punctured. A brain needle was used to localize the ventricle and it took 3 passes to localize the ventricle. The pressure was initially high. The CSF was clear and colorless. The CSF drainage rapidly tapered off because of the brain swelling. With two tries, the ventricular catheter was then able to be placed into the ventricle and then brought out through a separate puncture site; the depth of catheter was 7 cm from the outer table of the skull. There was intermittent drainage of CSF after that. The catheter was secured to the scalp with #2-0 silk sutures and the incision was closed with Ethilon suture. The patient tolerated the procedure well. No complications. Sponge and needle counts were correct. Blood loss is minimal.
     a. 61107, 62160
     b. 61210
     c. 61107
     d. 61210, 62160

113. Using the posterior approach the surgeon made a midline incision above the underlying vertebrae and dissected down to the paravertabral muscles and retracted then. The ligamentum flavum, lamina, and fragments of a ruptured C3-C4 intervertebral disc were all removed. The surgeon also removed a portion of the facet to relieve the compressed nerve of the C4 vertebrae. He then placed a free-fat graft over the exposed nerve and the paravertabral muscles were repositioned. The patient was then closed us-ing layered sutures and taken to recovery.

    a. 63040
    b. 63075
    c. 63081
    d. 63170

114. A procedure in which corneal tissue from a donor is frozen, reshaped and implanted into the anterior corneal stroma of the recipient to modify refractive error.

    a. 65710
    b. 65760
    c. 65765
    d. 65770

115. Which of the following organs is not part of the endocrine system

    a. Thyroid
    b. Pancreas
    c. Lymph Nodes
    d. Adrenal Glands

116. Using an operating microscope the ophthalmologist places stay sutures into the rectus muscle. A cold probe is then placed over the sclera and is depressed sealing the choroid to the retina at the original tear site. He then performs a sclerotomy and places mattress sutures across the incision. Subretinal fluid is then drained. Next a silicone sponge, followed by a silicone band, are placed around the eye and sutured into place to help support the healing scar. Rectus sutures are removed.

    a. 67101
    b. 671101, 69990
    c. 67107
    d. 67107, 69990

117. Following a motor vehicle collision a 28-year-old male was given a CT scan of the brain which indicated an infratentorial hematoma in the cerebellum. The patient was taken to the OR where the neurosurgeon, using the CT co-ordinates, incised the scalp and drilled a burr hole into the cranium above the hematoma. Under direct visualization he then evacuated the hematoma using suction and irrigated with NS. Hemorrhaging was controlled and the dura was closed. The skull piece was then placed back into the drill hole and screwed into place. The scalp was closed and the patient was sent to recovery.
    a. 61154
    b. 61253, 61315
    c. 61315
    d. 61154, 61315

118. An incision was made right in the mid palm area between the thenar and hypothenar eminence. Meticulous hemostasis of any bleeders was done. The fat was identified. The palmar aponeurosis was identified and cut and this was traced down to the wrist. There was severe compression of the median nerve. Additional removal of the aponeurosis was performed to allow for further decompression. After this was all completed, the area was irrigated with saline and bacitracin solution and closed as a single layer using Prolene 4-0 as interrupted vertical mattress stitches. Dressing was applied. The patient was brought to the recovery.
    a. 64702
    b. 64704
    c. 64719
    d. 64721

119. A postaurical incision is made on the right ear. With the use of an operating microscope the surgeon visualizes and reflects the skin flap and posterior eardrum forward. A small leak from the middle ear into the round window is noted. The surgeon then roughens up the surface of the window and packs it with fat. Upon retraction the eardrum and skin flap are replaced and the canal is packed. The surgeon then sutures the postaurical incision. He then repeats the procedure on the left ear.
    a. 69666-50, 69990
    b. 69667-50, 69990
    c. 69666, 69990
    d. 69667-50

120. Code 60512 should not be used:
    a. In conjunction with code 60260
    b. As a primary code
    c. As an additional code following a total thyroidectomy
    d. After code 60500

Radiology 70010 – 79999

121. Some radiology codes include two components. Often a radiologist will use the radiology equipment, which is known as the technical component, and the physician will provide the second half of the CPT code by supervising and interpreting the study. When this occurs what should the physician report?
    a. The full CPT code
    b. The CPT code with a modifier TC
    c. The CPT with a modifier 26
    d. The CPT with a modifier 52

122. A patient presents to the ER with intractable nausea and vomiting, and abdominal pain that radiates into her pelvis. The physician orders a CT scan of the abdomen, first without contrast and then followed by contrast, and a CT of the pelvis, without contrast.
    a. 74178
    b. 74178, 74176-51
    c. 74178 x2, 74177
    d. 74176, 74178-51

123. A patient was in an MVA and his face struck the steering wheel. He had multiple contusions and facial swelling. The physician suspected a zygomatic-malar or maxilla fracture. The radiologist took an oblique anterior-posterior projection, which showed the facial complex clearly. Anterior-posterior and lateral views were also taken.
    a. 70100
    b. 70120
    c. 70150
    d. 70250

124. If a prior study is available but it is documented in the medical records that there was inadequate visualization of the anatomy, then a diagnostic angiography may be reported in conjunction with an interventional procedure if modifier 59 is appended to the diagnostic S&I.
    a. True
    b. False

125. A physician performed a deep bone biopsy of the femur. The trocar was visualized and guided using a CAT scan and interpretation was provided.
    a. 20245, 77012-26
    b. 20225, 77012
    c. 38221, 76998
    d. 20225, 73700

126. HDR internal radiation therapy was performed by using a remote controlled MultiSource afterloader, which was connected to 3 catheters. The 6 Ir-192 radioactive wire sources were released from the containment unit and were delivered beside the tumor within the body cavity, as predetermined. After 15 minutes the sources were removed from the patient and placed back into the containment unit.
    a. 77762
    b. 77790
    c. 77771
    d. 77770

127. A patient has a myocardial perfusion imaging study which included quantitative wall motion, ejection fraction by gated technique and attenuation correction. The study was done during a cardiac stress test which was induced by using dipyridamole. The physician supervised, the interpretation and report were completed by the cardiologist.
    a. 78451, 93016
    b. 78453, 93016
    c. 78451
    d. 78453

128. A 35-year-old mother carrying twin gestations, who has a three-year-old child with Down syndrome, comes in for a prenatal screening. She is in her 12th week of pregnancy and the physician requests that the amount of fluid behind the necks of the fetuses be measured. A transabdominal approach was used.
    a. 76801, 76802
    b. 76811, 76812
    c. 76813, 76814
    d. 76816, 76816-59

129. A dialysis patient presents in the radiology department. His physician suspects that the tip of his Hickman's catheter in his left forearm may have migrated from its original placement. The vascular surgeon on-call injects radiopaque iodine into the patient's port and examines it under fluoroscopic imaging.
    a. 36598
    b. 36598, 75820
    c. 36598, 75820, 76000
    d. 75820

130. A written report signed by the interpreting physician should be considered an integral part of the radiological procedure or interpretation.
    a. True
    b. False

Pathology and Laboratory 80047 - 89398

131. A physician orders a patient's blood be tested for levels of urea nitrogen, sodium, potassium, transferase alanine and aspartate amnio, total protein, ionized calcium, carbon dioxide, chloride, creatinine, glucose, and TSH.
    a. 80053-52, 84443
    b. 80048, 84443, 84155, 84460, 84450
    c. 80047, 84460, 84450, 84155, 84443
    d. 80051, 84520, 84460, 84450, 84155,
       82330, 82565, 82947, 84443

132. A specimen labeled "right ovarian cyst" is received for examination. It consists of a smooth-walled, clear fluid filled cyst measuring 13x12x7 cm and weighing 1351 grams with fluid. Both surfaces of the wall are pink-tan, smooth and grossly unremarkable. No firm or thick areas or papillary structures are noted on the cyst wall externally or internally. After removal the fluid, the cyst weight 68 grams. The fluid is transparent and slightly mucoid.
    a. 88300
    b. 88304
    c. 88305
    d. 88307

133. A patient presents to the ED with chest pain, shortness of breath, and a history of congestive heart failure. The physician performs a 12 lead EKG which indicates a myocardial infarction without ST elevations. The physician immediately orders myoglobin, quantitative troponin, and CK enzyme levels to be run once every hour for three consecutive hours.
    a. 83874-99, 83874-76, 83874-91, 84484-99, 84484-76,
       84484-91, 82250-99, 82250-76, 82250-91
    b. 83874, 83874-91 x2, 84484, 84484-91 x2, 82550,
       82550-91 x2
    c. 83874-91 x3, 84484-91 x3, 82250-91 x3
    d. 83874 x3, 84484 x3, 82550 x3

134. A 17-year-old female presents in her family physician's office complaining of nausea, vomiting, and weight gain. She has been experiencing these symptoms on and off for two weeks. An analysis of the urine reveals a positive pregnancy test and hCG levels of 12500 mIU/ml confirm she is in her sixth week of pregnancy.
    a. 81005, 84702
    b. 81025, 84702
    c. 81025, 84703
    d. 81005, 84703

135. An employee was randomly selected for a drug screen. According to the employer it is standard procedure to use a multiplex screening kit, using non-TLC procedures, and test for barbiturates, cocaine, opiates and methadone. Any drug with a positive result should be confirmed with a second, definitive test. The employee showed positive for barbiturates and opiates. Secondary tests were run on the two and levels came back with 350 ng/ml for barbituates and 375 ng/ml for opiates.
    a. 80302, 80361, 80358
    b. 80301, 80361, 80358
    c. 80300 X4, 80345, 80361
    d. 80300, 80345, 80361

136. A CBC does not include which of the following:
    a. RBC
    b. Hgb
    c. hCG
    d. WBC

137. A couple that was unsuccessful at conceiving a child chooses to have in vitro fertilization done. The eggs and semen have been harvested and nine eggs were implanted with a sperm. The zygotes went through mitosis and produced embryos. Three embryos were then implanted in the woman and the other six were kept for later use. What codes(s) would the lab technician charge for her services in preserving the remaining six embryos?
    a. 89255 x6
    b. 89258
    c. 89268
    d. 89342

138. A patient in her 30th week of pregnancy has a high oral glucose reading and her physician orders a glucose tolerance test. Upon arrival the laboratory technician draws the patient's blood and the patient then ingests a glucose drink. Her blood is then drawn one, two and three hours after ingestion. As the patient was leaving the laboratory the technician informs her that the samples were incorrectly labeled and that the test needed to be repeated. The patient has her blood drawn again, ingested the glucose drink again, and has her blood redrawn at one, two and three hour intervals.
    a. 82951, 82951-91
    b. 82946, 82946-91
    c. 82947, 82950, 82950-91 x2
    d. 82951

139. Carbon dioxide, total calcium and sodium and all in what three panels?
    a. 82374, 82310, 84295
    b. 80069, 80047, 80048

140. A qualitative hCG test will provide a positive or negative result while a quantitative hCH test will provide a specific amount of hCG in the specimen.
    a. True
    b. False

Medicine 90281 - 99607

141. A 5 year old is brought into the ER after being attacked by a stray dog. The stray was captured and tested positive for rabies. The patient has a 3cm laceration on his right cheek that requires simple closure and a 1 cm and 4cm laceration on his upper left arm requiring layered repair. After discussing the benefits and risks with the patient's parents they decide to have an IM rabies vaccination administered by the physician, due to the patient's rabies exposure.
    a. S41.109A, S01.411A, Z23, 12013, 12031-51, 12032-51, 96372-51, 90375
    b. S41.112A, S01.411A, Z20.3, 12032, 12013-51, 90460-51, 90675
    c. S41.112A, S01.411A, Z23, 12032, 12013-51, 90471-51, 90675-51
    d. S41.112A, S01.411A, Z20.3, 12032, 12013-51, 90460-51, 90375

142. A 52-year-old man presents to the ER complaining of dizziness and fainting prior to arrival. The physician evaluates him, orders a 12 lead EKG and supervises the infusion of 2L of normal saline over 1 hour and 45 minutes, which is performed by a nurse.The EKG results are reviewed by the physician and found to be normal. The patient is diagnosed with syncope due to dehydration and released. In addition to the EM service what codes should be used for the doctor's services?
    a. 93010, 96360, 96361
    b. 93000, 96360
    c. 93010
    d. 93000, 96360, 96361

143. A 45-year-old patient with end stage renal disease has in home dialysis services initiated on the 15th of the month. The physician provides dialysis every day. On the 19th the patient was admitted to the hospital and discharged on the 24th. The physician and patient began in-home dialysis again on the 25th and continued every day until the 31st.
    a. 90960
    b. 90966
    c. 90970
    d. 90970 x11

144. A physician suspects his patient has left sided heart failure. To confirm his diagnosis, the doctor remotely monitors the patient's dual lead implantable cardioverter-defibrillator and the implantable cardiovascular monitor functionality within the patient's ICD over the course of 90 days. The physician analyzes recorded data from the device, including left atrial pressure, ventricular pressure and the patient's blood pressure. He also remotely analyzes data from the defibrillator, including heart rhythms and pace. There was one in-person interrogation of the ICM device and one in-person encounter for programming and adjusting the ICD device. The doctor reviews the data and compiles reports on both the ICD and the ICM.
    a. 93297 x3, 93295, 93290, 93283
    b. 93297, 93295, 93290, 93283
    c. 93297, 93295, 93283
    d. 93297 x3, 93295, 93283

145. **History:** Past ocular surgery history is significant for neurovascular age-related dry macular degeneration. Patient has had laser four times to the macula on the right and two times to the left.

    Exam: Established 63-year-old female patient. On examination, lids, surrounding tissues and palpebral fissure are all unremarkable. Conjunctiva, sclera, cornea and iris were all assessed as well. Palpitation of the orbital rim revealed nothing. Visual acuity with correction measured 20/400 OU. Manifest refraction did not improve this. There was no afferent pupillary defect. Visual fields were grossly full to hand motions. Intraocular pressure measured 17 mm in each eye. Vertical prism bars were used to measure ocular deviation and a full sensorimotor examination to evaluate the function of the ocular motor system was performed. A slit-lamp examination was significant for clear corneas OU. There was early nuclear sclerosis in both eyes. There was a sheet like 1-2+ posterior subcapsular cataract on the left. Dilated examination by way of cycloplegia showed choroidal neovascularization with subretinal heme and blood in both eyes. Magnified inspection was obtained with a Goldman 3-mirror lens and the retina, optic disc and retinal vasculature were visualized. Macular degeneration was present in both the left and right retinas.

    Assessment/Plan: Advanced neurovascular age-related macular degeneration OU, this is ultimately visually limiting. Cataracts are present in both eyes. I doubt cataract removal will help increase visual acuity; however, I did discuss with the patient, especially in the left, that cataract surgery will help us better visualize the macula for future laser treatment so that her current vision can be maintained. We discussed her current regimen and decided to continue with the high doses of the vitamins A, C and E, and the minerals zinc and copper to help slow her degeneration. After consideration, the patient agreed to left cataract surgery, which we scheduled for two weeks from today.
    a. 92012
    b. 92014
    c. 92014, 92060
    d. 92012, 92060, 92081

146. Some procedures or services are commonly carried out as an integral component of another total service or procedure and are identified by the inclusion term "separate procedure". Codes with this inclusion term should not be reported in addition to the total procedure code or service to which it is considered an integral part, unless it is independently carried out or considered unrelated. If performed independently or as an un-related procedure it may be coded with modifier 59 appended to it.
    a. True
    b. False

147. A 73-year-old group home resident with end stage renal disease has a nurse come in on Mondays, Wednesdays and Fridays to perform perito-neal dialysis. Each dialysis session lasts three hours. Once a week, (on Friday), the nurse also assists the patient with his meals, cleaning, and grocery shopping. What should the nurse charge for a month (30 days) of services if the 1st of the month landed on a Monday?
     a. 99601, 99602 x25, 99509 x4
     b. 99601 x13, 99602 x13, 99509 x4
     c. 90966, 99509 x4
     d. 99512 x 13, 99509 x4

148. The physician performs a non-imaging physiological recording of pres-sure on the left leg with Doppler analysis of blood flow in both directions. ABIs were taken at the back and front lower aspect of the tibial and tibial/dorsalis pedis arteries. In addition two levels of plethymography volume and oxygen tension were taken.
     a. 93923-52
     b. 93923
     c. 93922
     d. 93922-52

149. Due to a suspected gastric outlet obstruction, a manometric study is per-formed. Using nuclear medicine the physician monitors the time it takes for food to move through the patient's stomach, the time it take the pa-tient's stomach to empty into the small intestine and how fully it empties.
     a. 91010
     b. 91020
     c. 91022
     d. 91010, 91013

150. Which of the following drugs is not pending FDA approval?
     a. 90664
     b. 90666
     c. 90667
     d. 90668

CPC Practice Exam Answer Key With Rationale

Medical Terminology

1. **B** – The suffix -otomy means to cut into. Surgical removal is the suffix -ectomy. A permanent opening is the suffix -ostomy. Surgical repair is the suffix -plasty. Some CPT books have common medical terms like these listed in the first few pages.

2. **C** – Turn to the index in your CPT book and look up the term vaccination. Indented beneath *vaccination*, look for the abbreviation MMRV, or look up the term measles. You will see the full description "measles, mumps, rubella and varicella." Beneath it, you will see the abbreviation MMRV.

3. **D** – Each term listed can be found in the CPT book's index (if the term is not in the index, move to the next one). Beside the term "magnetic resonance imaging," you will see the abbreviation MRI.

4. **A** – Knowing medical terminology is useful here. The term "salp" means tube, while the term "ooph" refers to the ovary and the suffix -ectomy means "to surgically remove." Some CPT books have common medical terms like these listed in the first few pages of the book.

5. **D** – This is a rare instance in which the answer cannot be found in one of the medical coding books. I do know that this question (or one similar) often appears on the exam. I suggest writing out the meaning of this acronym in coding guidelines for the eyes/ears, just before the code sets (65091-69990), or in the notes section just after the code sets.

6. **C** – The prefix cryo- means cold, as in freezing.

7. D – The suffix –centesis means to puncture. Arthrocentesis is the puncturing and removal of fluid from a joint. Amniocentesis is the puncturing and removal of amniotic fluid from the amniotic sac during pregnancy. Pericardiocentesis is the puncturing of the pericardium a double-walled sac surrounding the heart and removal of excess fluid. paracentesis is the puncturing and removal of fluid from within a body cavity.

8. B – The medical prefix gastro- means stomach. The suffix –ectomy (option A) means "to remove." The suffix –otomy (option B) means to cut into. The suffix –ostomy (option C) means to create a permanent opening. The suffix –rrhaphy (option D) means to suture. Some CPT books have common medical terms like these listed in the first few pages.

9. **A** – The term nephro and the term renal both refer to the kidney. Examples: nephrolithasis (a kidney stone); renal calculi (a kidney stone).

10. **B** – The medical prefix myo- means muscle.

Anatomy

11. **A** – There are a few ways to look up anatomy questions. If your CPT book is issued by the AMA, and is either the professional or expert edition, then there is an anatomical chart for each organ system located with the coding guidelines for each number set, or within the Table of Contents for each number set. In this instance, a skeleton diagram is located in the Table of Contents for the musculoskeletal codes (20005-29999). If you do not have this diagram, try looking up the term "radius," either in the CPT or ICD-10-CM index and find a code or a few codes near that term. Flip to those codes and look for a diagram.

12. **B** – The answer to this question can be found using the same method described in the previous explanation.

13. **C** – Some CPT books will have a few diagrams located in the front of the book. These diagrams label body planes, regions, quadrants and directional terms (e.g. posterior). If your book does not contain these diagrams, try looking up "femur, fracture..." and then each term (distal, etc.) in the index. If the term does not appear in the index, that indicates that it is not the correct answer. Flip to the code provided for the terms that are in the index and look at any anatomical diagrams; e.g. "femur, fracture, distal" gives codes 27508, 27510 and 27514. If a diagram is not provided, remember that CPT codes are sequenced from the top of the body down, so code 27508 is closer to the hip (top of the body) and code 27514 is closer to the knee.

14. **A** – Look for an anatomical diagram in either the front of the CPT or in the guidelines of the digestive system. There are some anatomical diagrams in the HCPCS manual (2016) as well. Remember, the right side of the front of the human body appears on the left side of the diagram. You will see that the appendix is on the right side of the body. The sigmoid colon and descending colon are on the left side. The rectum is in the center of the body.

15. **B** – This is another occasion where you will either find the answer in the diagrams in the front of your CPT book or your book does not provide them. If you do not have these diagrams, this question will have to be an educated guess. Knowing medical terminology is beneficial here. In this case, the term "mid" means middle.

16. **D** – Prior to the digestive system coding guidelines, there is a diagram of the digestive system that labels the duodenum (where the stomach first empties into the small intestine), the Ileum and the Jejunum. The cecum is also labeled, but it is part of the large intestine.

17. **C** - The round window is located in the inner ear, while the oval window is located in the middle ear. Look up the term "round window" in the CPT index, and you will find code 69667 in the auditory system. Diagrams for code 69930 indicate the location of the round window.

18. **B** – Distal is the point of an organ or body part farthest from the point of attachment. The term "lateral" means "away from the midline of the body" and the term medial means "toward the midline of the body."

19. **C** – The temporalis is located in the jaw and helps move the tempromandubular joint. The trapezius muscle extends downward from the occipitalbone, along the thoracic vertebrae. The teres, deltoid and the four muscles that make up the rotator cuff are the six major muscles of the scapularhumeral group. The trigone muscle is a triangular smooth muscle sensitive to expansion and in charge of signaling to the brain when relief is needed.

20. **B** – The cardia fundus is the junction that joins the cardia (the top portion of the stomach closest to the heart) to the esophagus. The Latin term "fundus" applies to the portion of an organ opposite its opening. The cardia fundus is "opposite" the opening of the esophagus.

Coding Concepts

21. A -Just prior to code 22840 there are some code specific coding guidelines. The third paragraph states "do not append modifier 62 to spinal instrumentation codes 22840-22848 and 22850-22852."

22. B -ABN stands for "advanced beneficiary notice." It is a document that the patient signs stating that he or she will pay for the procedure being performed if insurance does not cover it. This is something taught in a medical billing or medical coding class, or something read in preparation for the exam. The answer is not in any of the coding books.

23. D -Wound exploration codes are 20100-20103. Directly above these codes are the wound exploration coding guidelines. These guidelines state that the following components are part of the codes description: surgical exploration and enlargement of the wound, extension of dissection, debridement, removal of foreign bodies, ligation or coagulation of minor subcutaneous and/or muscular blood vessel(s).

24. C -The CPT book contains two types of descriptions: common and unique. The common portion of a description follows the code, and ends with a semicolon (;). Any CPT sharing that description will be indented beneath the code. Descriptors following the semicolon (;) are unique to a that specific code. Code 24900 contains the common descriptor "Amputation, arm through humerus." Codes 24920 through 24931 share that descriptor, so they are indented underneath with their unique descriptor beside them.

25. C -Medical necessity is what adjudicates or justifies a claim for payment. If a physician wants to be paid for a laceration repair (CPT), the ICD-10 code used should describe a situation that says it is necessary (the ICD-10 code should be a laceration or open wound).

26. C -Answer C is false since ICD-10-CM Guideline I.C.20.a.2 instructs coders to assign an external cause code, with the appropriate seventh character (initial encounter, subsequent encounter or sequela) for each encounter. Answer A is true, since External Causes of Morbidity (Chapter 20 codes) are listed in the V01-Y99 range in the Tabular. Answer B is true: according to ICD-10-CM Guideline I.C.20.a.4, which says to "Assign as many external cause codes as necessary to fully explain each cause." Answer D is true, according to Guideline I.C.20.a.6, which dictates that an external cause code can never be a principal, or first-listed, diagnosis.

27. **D** – Appendix E lists all CPT codes that are modifier 51 exempt. Beside each code in the tabular there is a convention that looks like a circle with a backslash through it. This convention means that the code next to it is modifier 51 exempt. Code 45392 is the only code not listed in appendix E and does not have this convention beside it.

28. **A** – Category III codes are located between the Category II codes and Appendix A in the back of the CPT manual. Category III coding guidelines state that these codes are to be used before assigning an unlisted procedure code from category I codes.

29. **D** – Medicare Part A is hospital insurance, and helps cover inpatient care in hospitals, skilled nursing facilities, hospices and home healthcare. Medicare Part B helps cover medically necessary services like doctors' services, outpatient care, home health services and other medical services. It also covers some preventative services.

30. **D** – HIPAA has three rules: privacy, security and patient safety. Standards for transmitting PHI are not regulated by HIPAA, but the security of this information while it is being transmitted is. Once transmission rules are set, HIPAA then sets the standards for how this information should be protected.

ICD-10-CM

31. **D** – The question specifies stage 3 kidney disease, so it is referring to "chronic" kidney disease. In the ICD-10-CM index, search for Disease/kidney/ hypertensive, which points to Hypertension, kidney. Search for Hypertension, kidney with stage 1 through stage 4 chronic kidney disease, and you will find 112.9. In the Tabular, 112.9 is Hypertensive chronic kidney disease with stage 1 through stage 4 chronic kidney disease, or unspecified chronic kidney disease. The Tabular directs you to use additional code to identify the stage of chronic kidney disease. The correct code is N18.3 Chronic kidney disease, stage 3 (moderate).

32. **D** – The principal diagnosis should be for the laceration to her left forearm. In the ICD- 10-CM Index, look up Laceration, forearm, left, with foreign body, which is code S51.822. A seventh digit is needed, which is A, for initial encounter. Code S51.812A, or Laceration without foreign body of left forearm, is incorrect because the laceration has embedded glass. This eliminates answers A and C. In the External Causes Index, look up Fall, falling (accidental) from chair, which is code W07. Again, a seventh digit is needed, which is A. Code W18.02XA, striking against glass with subsequent fall, is incorrect because in the case study, the patient's fall occurred first, followed by her striking against the glass stovetop. At this point, the answer is clearly D. To find the additional codes, look up Contact with glass (broken), which indicates W25. Again, a seventh digit is needed, which is A. According to ICD-10-CM guideline I.C.20.c, "an activity code should be used in conjunction with a place of occurrence code, Y92," so the correct answer requires activity and place of occurrence codes. Activity codes are Y93 codes. Under Y93 in the ICD-10-CM manual, there is a list we can scan to find that Y93.E codes are for Activities involving personal hygiene and interior property and clothing maintenance. Checking the Tabular, Y93.E9, or Activity, other interior property and clothing maintenance, is the appropriate code. For place of occurrence, the code Y92.030 covers residence, apartment, kitchen. According to Guideline I.C.20.b, place of occurrence codes are listed after other external cause codes.

33. **B** – Burn codes always have at least three codes: A burn code, a total body surface area code, or T31 category code, and an external cause code. Burn codes have the following rules, which can be found at the beginning of the ICD-10-CM manual under Guideline I.C.19.d Coding of burns and corrosions. Always code one location to the highest degree. For example, for first and second degree burns on the arm, you would only code second degree. When sequencing burn codes, always list the highest degree burn code first and end with the lowest degree burn code. For example, regarding first degree burns to the face and third degree burns to the arm, you would list the arm burn first and then the face burn. For question 33, answer B is correct because its codes describe the highest degree burn to each location and the burn codes are also arranged the in the correct order of highest to lowest degree of burn. To find the codes for the actual burns, we start with the areas with the third degree burns, in this case the face and thigh burns. Look up Burn/ face, and you will find Burn/ head. Burn, head, third degree is

T20.30-. Search for Burn, thigh, third degree and you will find T24.319-. The second degree burns are for the upper and forearms. In the index, Burn, arm points to Burn, upper, limb. Looking up Burn, upper limb, multiple sites to code for both the upper arm and forearm, you will find that second degree is T22.299-. All of these need seven characters, with the seventh character being A, for initial encounter. The T31.42 (TBSA code) has the correct calculation when using the rule of nine (fourth digit burned to any degree; 9 x 5 = 45; five areas burned are head, arm1, arm2, leg1, leg 2; 5th digit describes only 3rd degree burns which are head (9), leg1 (9), and leg2 (9). 9 x 3 = 27). To find the code using the index, look up Burn, extent 40-49 percent with 20-29 percent third degree burns which points to T31.42. The external cause code correctly describes the bonfire incident. In the External Causes Index, look up Exposure, fire, not in building or structure which designates code X03.0. This also requires a seventh character of A, making the code X03.0XXA. Verify all codes in the Tabular.

34. **D** - Options B and C can be excluded because of code O80, which describes a normal - not prolonged - delivery. Code O63.0 is correct for prolonged labor during the first stage. Option A contains the code O09.519 Supervision of elderly primigravida, unspecified trimester, which is not correct because the pregnancy is in the 38th week, which is the third trimester. Code O09.513 is the correct code for Supervision of elderly primigravida, third trimester. The code Z37.0, single liveborn, is correct.

35. **A** - The patient presents with pain in his distal middle finger. Look up Fracture, traumatic, finger, middle, distal phalanx (displaced) in the ICD-10-CM Index, which leads to S62.63-. Note that there is no entry under Fracture for tuft fracture. Tuft means a fracture of the distal phalanx. According to the Tabular, S62.632A would be the correct code for displaced fracture of distal phalanx of right middle finger. This eliminates B and C. In the External Causes Index, look up Activity, baseball which denotes Y93.64 and eliminates option D. Find the other codes by looking up Bumping against, into (accidentally) person(s) which would be W51, so the correct code would be W51.XXXA, because it needs a seventh character. Look up Place of Occurrence, sports area, athletic, field, baseball which indicates Y92.320. Note that the documentation did not state that the collision with the other player caused a fall, so code W03.XXXA would be incorrect.

36. **B** - Alcohol and drug abuse are both considered less severe than dependence, since abuse can be stopped voluntarily. However, abuse usually escalates to dependence. Dependence is defined as "when one cannot voluntarily stop." It is critical to pay attention to whether the documentation indicates abuse or dependence. Since the patient cannot

voluntarily stop using amphetamines on his own, this is a case of dependence. The documentation mentions both alcohol abuse and alcoholism, so alcohol dependence must be coded. In the ICD-10-CM Index, look up Dependence, amphetamine(s) and it points to Dependence, drug, stimulant NEC. Upon searching, we are directed to F15.20, or Other stimulant dependence, uncomplicated. This eliminates option C, which does not contain the code F15.20. Note that there is an Excludes1 note, which prevents us from coding F15.10 (Other stimulant abuse, uncomplicated) with F15.20 (other stimulant dependence). This eliminates options A and D. Now we know that the answer is option B. The other codes can be found by looking up "Alcoholism" or "Dependence, alcohol," which directs to F10.20; also Anxiety, generalized, which points to F41.1, and Disorder, post-traumatic stress, which leads to F43.10: Post-traumatic stress disorder, unspecified.

37. **C** - In the ICD-10-CM Index, look up Diabetes, with retinopathy, which leads to E11.319. Checking the Tabular, E11.319 is the code for Type 2 diabetes mellitus with unspecified diabetic retinopathy without macular edema. There is a note to use additional code to identify any insulin use, Z79.4, for E11. Insulin use was not mentioned in the documentation, so we cannot code it. Option A, E08.319: DM due to underlying condition with unspecified diabetic retinopathy without macular edema, is incorrect because the documentation does not state that the DM is is due to an underlying condition. Option B, E11.311: Type 2 DM with unspecified diabetic retinopathy with macular edema is incorrect because macular edema is not mentioned.

38. **A** - This is true according the ICD-10-CM coding guidelines, found in the beginning of the manual. Section I.B.5 says that "Signs and symptoms that are associated routinely with a disease process should not be assigned as additional codes, unless otherwise instructed by the classification."

39. C - ICD-10-CM coding guidelines, found in the beginning of the manual, stipulate the HIV coding rules in Section I.C.1.a. These guidelines state that Z21 should be coded for asymptomatic HIV (HIV with no documented symptoms) and may include the terms "HIV positive," "known HIV," and "HIV test positive." There are also extensive notations in the tabular portion beneath each of the HIV codes. Beneath code B20 is an Excludes1 notation stating that this code excludes asymptomatic HIV and to see code Z21. Code R75 is used for inconclusive laboratory evidence of HIV. Beneath code R75 is an Excludes1 notation stating this code excludes asymptomatic HIV and to see code Z21. Code B97.35 is used for HIV, type 2 as the cause of diseases classified elsewhere.

40. A - According to ICD-10-CM Guideline I.C.19.d (first paragraph), solar radiation burns are sunburns and are coded differently than other thermal burns. In the ICD- 10-CM Index, look up Sunburn, second degree, which directs you to L55.1, which is the correct code. The other, incorrect code choices are L56.8: Other specified acute skin changes due to ultraviolet radiation, T21.23XA: Burn of 2nd degree of upper back, initial encounter, and L58.92: Radiodermatitis, unspecified.

HCPCS

41. **C** – Options A and D can be eliminated when comparing codes A6204 and A6252. Code A6204 states composite dressing is used, while code A6252 states special absorptive sterile dressing is used (which is correct). When choosing between options B and C, code A6219 meets the correct size requirements and also has an adhesive border.

42. **D** – Option A is a plaster cast, so it is incorrect. Option B is for a pediatric cast (0-10 years). Since the patient is 12, this code is also incorrect. Option C meets most of the description, but it is for a splint rather than a cast. Option D meets all the requirements of short arm cast, adult (11 years +) and made from fiberglass.

43. **C** – The correct answer is C (J9070). Neosar directs you to Cyclophosphamide 100 mg, which is a Chemotherapy drug used intravenously. Answer A for J9100 is for Cytarabine 100 mg, which is not the correct medication. Answer B (J7502) is for Cyclosporine oral medication, which is an immunosuppressive drug. Answer D is J8999 and is a prescription oral chemotherapeutic drug, and this patient is getting IV infusion.

44. **B** – The title for each code range is listed at the beginning of its code sets. Example: B codes start with code B4034 and right before this code is the B code set title "Enteral and Parenteral Therapy (B4034-B9999)." By turning to the first code in each code set listed you can locate the titles. Note that there is a difference between orthopedic footware and Diabetic footwear.

45. **B** – Code E1222 is the only option that specifies elevating leg rests (but not the detachable and swing away style). Although the other codes describe similar chairs, we cannot code for something unless it is explicitly stated. You should also not assume that a "heavy duty wheelchair" or "high strength wheelchair" is needed because of the patient's size.

E/M

46. **C** - Notice first that this question provides no key components, so we can eliminate any code with key component requirements. Aside from the key components, option A can be eliminated because it describes a new patient. This patient comes in weekly, which means she is established. Option B requires key components that are not provided in this question, so this can be eliminated as well. Option D describes a code used for a patient on blood thinners, and is described in detail in the coding guidelines right above it. Code 99211 is listed under established patients and is one of the only codes in this section that a physician cannot use. This code is used for ancillary staff only (e.g. LPN, MA), which would apply in this instance, since an LPN saw the patient. The description of this code also gives a hint, as it states that this code is for visits that are "typically 5 minutes."

47. **D** - Options A and and C are incorrect because the observation codes listed here (99218) are only for patients who are admitted and discharged on two different dates. Option B is incorrect because the description beneath this code states that it requires three key components: "Comprehensive history, comprehensive exam, and moderate MOM." The physician performed only a detailed history and exam (not a comprehensive exam). Although his MOM was of moderate complexity, he did not provide the other two key components at the comprehensive level. Since the requirement of code 99235 is for all three key components to be met, option B is also incorrect. Option O is correct because codes 99234-99236 are used for patients who were admitted and discharged on the same day (see coding guidelines directly above code 99234). Code 99234 also requires that all 3 key components be met. In this scenario the first two key components (history and exam) met the requirement of being "detailed." The third key component (MOM) was also met and exceeded. Since the physician went beyond straightforward/ low complexity MOM and went to moderate MOM, code 99234 may be used.

48. **D** - Code 99471 applies to this case, eliminating answers A and C, since it covers initial critical care for an inpatient pediatric, aged 29 days to 24 months. This narrows the choices to B and D. B is incorrect because it includes a code for intubation, 31500. The ICD-10-CM code R06.89 in B is also incorrect because it does not include the "acute" status. IC0-10-CM code J80 accurately describes acute respiratory distress and code J18.9 describes pneumonia, unspecified organism.

CPC Practice Exam Answer Key with Rationale

49. **D** – The physician performed three services: stand by, resuscitation and an E/M. Reading the descriptions of these codes and the guidelines provided for each code to determine which of them can or cannot be code in conjunction with each other. The coding guidelines for code 99360 state that the code "should not be used if the period of standby ends with the performance of a procedure." It may seem that this would then rule out the use of this code, since Dr.Smith did render a procedure (resuscitation). However, there is a special notation in parentheses beneath code 99360 that states "99360 may be reported in addition to 99460, 99465 as appropriate." The next CPT code 99465 describes newborn resuscitation in the delivery room. This was the procedure that Dr. Smith provided, and is correct. The last code is 99460. This code describes the new born E/M that the physician provided. This code has no special notations or exclusions and is also correct. There is also a notation beneath code 99465 that states "99465 may be reported in conjunction with 99460." This means that all three codes can be used together.

50. **D** – Compare code 99387 to 99397. Both are for an annual wellness exam, and according to their descriptions, include age/gender-appropriate history, exam, counseling (e.g. smoking cessation), guidance, risk factors, etc. Code 99387 is for a new patient, however, and 99397 is for an *established* patient (both state the correct age). Since Mr. Johnson is an established patient, options A and B can be eliminated because of code 99387 (new patient). For options C and D, compare codes 99205 and 99215. Both of these codes describe an in-office E/M with a primary care physician. Code 99205 is for a new patient and also requires that all three key components be met. This code is incorrect because the patient is *established* (not new), and the MDM provided was only of moderate complexity (this code requires high complexity MDM). Even though code 99215 is for an established patient, and the MDM for this code states High while the physician only provided Moderate, the code description states that only two of the three key components need to be met. Since the Comprehensive history and exam were met, this code can still be assigned. This means option D, which includes both 99397 and 99215, is correct.

© 2011-2016 http://www.medicalbillingandmedicalcoding.com   101

51. C – The answer to this question is found in the E/M coding guidelines under the 9th heading, labeled "Levels of E/M Service." These guidelines, along with the guidelines found in this section under the heading "Time,"explain that the 6 components 1) History 2) Exam 3) Medical Decision Making 4)Counseling 5) Coordination of Care 6) Nature of Presenting Problem or time (by itself), determines the level of an E/M service.

52. C – A 13-month-old child is over a year old, so this rules out option B. Option C is more specific than option A, and meets our description. Option D is incorrect because it does not describe a hernia repair, but repair of the backside of the abdominal wall.

53. A – The terms diagnostic and arthroscopic point to answer A. While answer B provides the correct anatomical description, this is also for an actual procedure (e.g., surgery), and not considered exploratory for diagnostic purposes. Answer C describes an arthroscopic procedure, but it is also for a surgery (not diagnostic). Answer D describes the actual procedure that the surgeon performed, but we are only coding the anesthesia for the anesthesiologist in this scenario.

Anesthesia

54. **C** – The answer to this question is located in the Anesthesia coding guidelines under the title "Time Reporting."

55. **B** – The lining surrounding the heart is called the pericardium. Knowing this narrows the options. Code 00560 accurately describes the surgery that was performed, but this code is meant to be used for patients over the age of one, and does not include the oxygenator pump. Code 00561 in option B states that this code is for children under on year of age, and includes an oxygenator pump. When the age is specified in the code's description, it is not necessary to add a qualifying circumstance code (99100), restating the extreme age. Directly beneath code 00561, there is a notation stating "Do not report 00561 in conjunction with 99100, 99116, and 99135." This eliminates option D. Option C is incorrect because it does not describe surgery on the pericardium, but on the great vessels of the heart.

56. **C** - By recognizing the patient's age, you can narrow your options to A or C (because of the qualifying circumstance code 99100 depicts extreme age, applying patients under the age of 1 and over the age of 70). Qualifying circumstance codes can also be located in the Anesthesia coding guidelines, and/or in the medicine chapter. Knowing medical terminology will also help to eliminate options in this question. Option A describes a teno*tomy*; the suffix -otomy means to cut into, or to make an incision. Option B describes a teno-*desis*. The suffix –*esis* means to remove fluid. In this question, a repair was being performed. Code 01714 uses the term tenoplasty. The suffix –plasty means to repair. Option C and D provide the same code, but D does not list the qualifying circumstance code 99100. Also the P modifier for severe asthma is P3.

57. B – The answer to this question is found in the bottom half of paragraph two in the Anesthesia coding guidelines.

58. A – The qualifying circumstance codes (99140) is correct and narrows the choice to options A or D. Both A and D have the same P modifier (P5), which is correct. Codes P5 and 99140 are correct because the patient is hemorrhaging and will bleed out and die without the operation; the surgery is also stated as "emergency." Option D describes an unspecified code, but option A describes a tubal ligation, including laparoscopic procedures, which is what this scenario describes.

59. D – This question can be narrowed down by either the P modifier, or by knowing the medical terminology. The P1 modifier describes an otherwise healthy individual, while P2 describes an individual with a mild systemic disease (P modifiers are listed in Appendix A with all other modifiers). Since this patient was stated as "healthy," we can choose P1, which will narrow the options to A or D. Option A is close, but unspecified. Option B describes an – otoscopy, which is the use of a scope in the ear. Option C describes biopsies of intraoral locations, and the term oral indicates the mouth. Answer D describes a biopsy (-otomy) of the eardrum (tympanum).

60. D – According to the Anesthesia coding guidelines under the heading "Time Reporting," anesthesia time begins when the anesthesiologist begins preparing the patient for the induction of anesthesia and ends when the anesthesiologist releases the patient from his care and is no longer in attendance. In this question, this means the anesthesia time is from 8:15 am through 9:30 am, or 1 hour and 15 minutes.

61. A - When facing a long and complex question like this one, it help to eliminate some of the options. To eliminate two of the four choices, determine which P status modifier is correct, P2 or P3, or compare codes S52.501A and S52.501 B, since each of these appears in two of the four answers. In this case, the P2 status modifier is correct since both systemic diseases (diabetes and asthma) are well controlled and mild. The diagnosis code S52.501A is correct because the fracture is not described as open, only the procedure is open. Unless it is explicitly stated that a fracture is open or closed, it is assumed to be closed, according to ICD-10-CM guideline I.C.19.c, second paragraph. This means code S52.501A (where the 7th character means initial encounter for closed fracture) is correct. This eliminates both B and D. To decide between choices A and C, look up anesthesia codes 01830 and 01810. Code 01810 describes procedures for nerves, muscles, tendons, fascia and the bursa, but not the bone. Code 01830 is correct because it covers procedures performed on the distal radius bone, either open or with a scope. Additional ICD-10-CM codes E11.9 for Type 2 diabetes mellitus without complications and J45.909 for Unspecified asthma, uncomplicated are also correct. The ICD-10-CM codes Z86.39 for Personal history of other endocrine, nutritional and metabolic disease and Z87.09 for Personal history of other diseases of circulatory system are not specific enough for this case.

Integumentary

62. B - According to the laceration coding guidelines above code 12001, multiple lacerations located in the same anatomical group that require the same depth of repair may have their lengths added together for a single code selection. Since the 2.5cm and 4cm lacerations are both on the arm and share the same depth that requires layered lacerations, their lengths can be added together to get 6.5 cm. The correct code is therefore 12032, since it meets the criteria of depth, length and location. The 3cm facial laceration gets a separate CPT code because of its depth and location. Code 12013 is correct here, since it meets the criteria. According to the laceration repair guidelines, when more than one classification of wound is repaired, the coder must list the more complicated wound as the primary procedure and the less complicated wound as the secondary procedure, using modifier 59. Answer B correctly sequences the codes and has an appended 59 modifier. In the ICD-10-CM Index, Wound, open, forearm indicates code S51.80-. The full code is S51.802A for left side, initial encounter. Wound, open, shoulder points to S41.00-. The full code is S41.001A for right side, initial encounter. Laceration, forehead specifies code S01.81-. The full code is S01.81XA, Laceration without foreign body of other part of head, initial encounter.

63. C - The removal of lesions is determined by type. Benign and premalignant lesions have one set of removal codes, while malignant lesion removal has another set of codes. Each set of codes is further divided by anatomical grouping, size and the number of lesions being removed. In this case, the benign lesion on the scalp and premalignant lesion on the neck will be coded with codes 17000-17250. The malignant lesion of the hand will be coded using codes 17260-17286. Sequencing these codes from most severe to least severe, code the malignant ablation first, followed by premalignant and finally the benign ablation. Code 17273 is accurate because it is listed under the heading "destruction, malignant lesions, any method." The anatomical grouping starts at code 17270 (and includes the hand), and the specific code 17273 describes the size range 2.1 cm – 3.0 cm. Since our malignant growth was 2.5cm, this code is correct. The premalignant growth and benign growth are coded under the same heading "Destruction Benign or Premalignant Lesions" (code range 17000 - 17250). Code 1700 describes the removal of the premalignant lesion only, and does not include benign lesions. There is no anatomical grouping here, just codes for the number of lesions being destroyed. Code 17003 is an add-on code that should only be used in conjunction with code 17000 (see notation beneath code 17003). This code should not be used with just another lesion destruction code (e.g. 17273 & 17003). Code 17110 is used to describe the removal of the benign lesion of any location, up to 14.

64. **D** – When faced with multiple codes that are similar, there are two ways to determine the correct code. Either choose the code that provides the most detail and remains accurate, or look up the terms in the alphabetic index. In this case look up the terms "breast, cyst, puncture aspiration" in the index. This will lead you to the code set 19000-19001. Code 19000 provides the most detail because it has a specific anatomical location along with the correct description (a puncture aspiration).

65. **A** – The simplest way to determine precisely what was done during this procedure is to look at the information at the very end of the operative note. Here we have the information that is most important to us: simple linear closure was performed; two stages (described as Mohs), were performed, and the number of sections in each stage is reported. According to the Mohs microsurgery guidelines, repairs are not bundled into the procedure and can be billed additionally. This means that the repair code 12002 (simple repair, 6.5 cm, scalp) is correct. We can eliminate options C and D. Options A and B share three of the same codes, with one additional code in option A. The question is do you need code 17315? Going through the Stages and Sections: Stage I Section 1-5 is coded with 17311; Stage I Section 6 is coded with 17315; Stage II Section 1-5 (only 2 sections were performed in this scenario) is coded with 17312. Code 12002 describes the simple, 3.5 cm closure of the scalp.

66. **C** – What the surgeon performed is a split-thickness graft. A split-thickness graft uses the epidermis and a portion of the dermis from healthy tissue, removes it from its original location, but leaves a portion of it connected. The point of connection keeps the dermis and epidermis alive and is used as the pivot point for the graft. Option A describes something similar, but this is an adjacent tissue transfer (e.g. flap graft), which is usually thicker than a split-thickness graft, and usually involves the transfer of underlying tissues. Option B describes an autograft. An autograft can come from a donor site or from skin that is grown in a laboratory from the patient's own cells and later grafted to the defective area. Option D describes a flap graft, which is deeper than just the dermis and can be rotated around a point, as opposed to just being flipped over.

67. **A** – For this question read each code's specific coding guidelines in order to determine which services are bundled. The 64400 code describes a digital block, but this code would not be used because digital blocks are already built into the reimbursement for a laceration code and/or a subungual hematoma evacuation. This eliminates option B. Code 20103 states in the guidelines that this code is only used when a penetrating trauma has occurred, and this injury is not penetrating. In addition, this code describes extensive debridement, wound enlargement, major vessel ligation, etc. Minor debridement, ligation and exploration are already bundled into a laceration repair code(see laceration coding guidelines), and since the question does not state that anything above routine (minor) work was done, we cannot use code 20103.This eliminates options B, C and D. By Option A is the only choice left remaining. HCPCS modifiers F6 and F7 are correctly used to depict each individual finger. These modifiers can be found in Appendix A. Code 12042 accurately describes a layered finger laceration of 3 cm, and code 11740 accurately describes a subungual hematoma evacuation.

68. **B** – According to the lesion excision coding guidelines (above code set 11400-11471) "Code selection is determined by measuring the greatest clinical diameter of the apparent lesion plus that margin required for complete excision (lesion diameter plus the most narrow margins required equals the excised diameter)."

69. **A** – True. According to the laceration "Repair (closure)"coding guidelines (above code 12001), under the heading "Definitions, intermediate repair," "Single-layer closure of heavily contaminated wounds that have required extensive cleaning or removal of particulate matter also constitutes intermediate repair."

70. **C** – Knowing the medical terminology involved will help determine the answer here. The prefix auto- means "self." Hence, an autograft is a graft in which the donor skin is from a different site on the recipient's body. The medical prefix a- means "without," and the term cell refers to living cells. "Acellular graft" (a- and cell) translates "without human cells," because it is made of synthetic materials. The medical prefix allo- means "other". In "allograft," the prefix allo- refers to a graft from another human being. Finally, the prefix xeno- means "foreign." Xenograft refers to a graft from a foreign species (e.g. pig).

71. **C** – Code 97597 and 97602 are found in the medicine chapter and describe active open wound care (e.g. decubitus ulcers). Beneath the Active Wound Care Management coding guidelines there is the notation "For debridement of burn wounds, see 16020-16030." This eliminates options A and B. Code 16030 is used to describe the removal of dead tissue on second-degree (partial thickness) burns. Not only is the degree of burn different, but in this scenario, there is no mention of tissue removal, only cleansing and incisions. This eliminates option D. Code 16035 describes an Escharotomy (note the suffix –otomy means to "cut into"). An Escharotomy is a procedure performed on healing third degree burns. Incisions are made into the thick dead tissue to keep underlying nerves and vessels from being injured or constricted. Code 16036 is an add-on code used in conjunction with code 16035. This add-on code should be used for each additional incision. So code 16035 describes the first incision, while code 16036 x2 describes the second and third incision.

Musculoskeletal

72. **D** - Option A describes an open rather than arthroscopic procedure, so this option can be eliminated. Option B is arthroscopic, but the procedure is a transplant (instead of a repair), so this too is incorrect. The difference between C and D is the word "and" vs. "or." In this question, the patient had both the medial and lateral meniscus repaired, so code 29883 is correct.

73. **B** - Open fractures do not necessarily use open fracture treatment codes. In the ICD-10- CM, an open fracture means that the skin is broken. In the CPT book, "open" and "closed" refer to treatment type. If a patient is taken to the operating room and an incision is made to see the fracture, it is considered open treatment. A physician manipulating a fracture without creating an opening is performing a closed treatment. In this case, the patient has an open fracture, but the treatment is closed. Code 25574 describes an open treatment, so answers A and C are wrong. Answers B and D both have the correct CPT codes, but use different modifiers. A procedure with a 90 global period can be broken down into pre-operative assessment and decision for surgery; surgical - the procedure- and post-operative follow-up care. In this case, the fracture care has a 90 global period so it can be broken down. The EM, or pre-operative part, should have the 57 modifier appended. The 57 modifier describes decision for surgery, as seen in appendix A. The 25 modifier is also appended to the EM because of the additional procedure - 12031, laceration repair. The fracture reduction and sutures require that modifier 54 be appended to the fracture care code. Modifier 54 is for surgical care only, as seen in appendix A. The HCPCS modifier RT is used to indicate which arm was treated. See appendix A for the RT modifier's full description. The ICD-10-CM code is found by looking up Fracture, radius, lower end in the Index, which points to code S52.50-. The full code is S52.501 B for Unspecified fracture of the lower end of right radius, initial encounter for open fracture NOS.

74. **D** - Knowing medical terminology will help find the answer to this question. Specific medical suffixes usually fall under a specific heading (e.g. the suffix -otomy, which means to "cut into," is usually under the heading "incisions"). The suffix -ectomy, which means "to remove," is usually found under the "excision" heading. The suffixes -plasty and -pexy mean to re-pair, so terms with these suffixes usually fall under the heading "repair;" Scapulopexy, for example. If you do not know the medical terminology, you can try looking up the term scapulopexy in the index. This will lead you to code 23400. Code 23400 is under the heading "Repair, Revision, and/or Reconstruction."

75. **B** – The procedure being performed in this scenario is a trigger point injection. Codes 64400 and 64520 are used to describe nerve blocks. These are injections involving the nervous system, instead of injecting muscles, as was done in this scenario. Options A and C can be eliminated. Codes 20552 and 20553 both describe trigger point injections, and both codes include multiple injections. Code 20552 describes 1 or more injections into 1 – 2 muscles, and code 20553 describes 1 or more injections into 3 or more muscles. Since only one muscle was being injected multiple times, code 20552 is correct.

76. **A** – Per Paul Cadorette and the American Medical Association article "Coding Guidance for Anterior Cervical Arthrodesis," "When a spinal fusion (arthrodesis) is performed, the first thing a coder needs to recognize is the approach or technique that was utilized. With an anterior (front of the body) approach to a cervical fusion the incision will be made in the patient's neck, so the key terms to look for are platysma, esophagus, carotid and sternocleidomastoid. These structures will be divided and/or protected during dissection down to the vertebral body. After dissection, the procedure can proceed in one of three ways:
a. When the interspace is prepared (minimal discectomy, perforation of endplates) then 22554 would be reported.
b. When a discectomy is performed to decompress the spinal cord and/or nerve root(s) report 22554 for the arthrodesis along with 63075 for the discectomy procedure.
c. When a partial corpectomy (vertebral body resection) is performed at C5 and C6 report CPT code 22554 for the arthrodesis with 63081 and 63082. Two codes are reported because the corpectomy procedure is performed on two vertebral segments (C5 and C6). CPT codes 63081-63091 include a discectomy above and/or below the vertebral segment, so code 63075 (discectomy) would not be reported if performed at the C5-C6 interspace.

Once the decompression procedure has been completed, a PEEK cage can be placed within the interspace or a structural bone graft can be fashioned to fit the vertebral defect created by the previous corpectomy. Insertion of the PEEK cage would be reported with a biomechanical device code 22851. This code is only reported one time per level even if two cages are placed at C5-C6. When a structural bone graft is used, determine whether it is an allograft (20931) or an autograft (20938). The bone graft codes are only reported one time per procedure and not once for each level. Finally, the physician will place an anterior plate with screws (22845) across the C5-C6 interspace to stabilize the area of fusion". Guidance on coding such procedures can also be located in the Spine (vertebral column) coding guidelines (above code 22010).

77. B – In this scenario each answer has the identical codes, but with different modifiers. Modifiers can be referenced quickly on the front cover of the CPT book, and can be found along with a full description and guidelines in Appendix A. Guidance for this question comes from looking at the guidelines above the two codes that were provided. According to osteotomy guidelines (above code 22206), when two surgeons work together as primary surgeons performing distinct parts of an anterior spine osteotomy, each surgeon should report his or her distinct operative work by appending modifier 62 to the procedure code.

78. D – "Fracture care," as described by code 25600, includes pain management, fracture reduction (if necessary), and initial stabilization. Since the patient came into the physician's office with a cast already in place, we can deduce that the patient already received initial fracture care. Coding 25600 would be inappropriate, because the patient was already charged for fracture care once. The physician performed only a cast application, as described by code 29075. Option C is also incorrect. Although the physician did remove the prior cast, it was never specified a "full arm cast," and was most likely a short arm cast, but you cannot draw assumptions when coding.

79. D – According to arthroscopy coding guidelines (found above code 29800), surgical arthroscopies include diagnostic arthroscopies. They are bundled, so this means that a diagnostic arthroscopy cannot be billed in conjunction with a surgical arthroscopy. If a diagnostic arthroscopy turns into a surgical procedure, the surgeon can only bill for the surgical portion. This eliminates code 29805, which appears on both options A and B. Code 29819 has the correct description for removal of a foreign body in the shoulder by arthroscopy. Modifier 78 would not be appended because the patient is past his 90 day global period, and there is no mention that this is the same surgeon who performed the initial surgery.

80. **B** – Most CPT books (like the one published by the AMA and required by the AAPC for the CPC Exam) have diagrams with detailed descriptions accompanying these codes. If your CPT book has their diagrams, reading the detailed captions will direct you to the correct code selection. In this scenario, the diagram provided for code 28290 describes the correct "medial eminence of the metatarsal bone" being removed. Since there is no mention of the Kirschner wire used to stabilize the joint, however, this code is incorrect. The diagram for code 28294 describes a bunionectomy, but describes a tendon transplant being an integral component of this procedure. This was not performed in this scenario. The diagram for code 28298 describes the removal of the "medial eminence" and the Kirschner wire stabilization, but also includes the removal of several bone wedges from the base of the phalanx. This scenario describes the surgeon cutting into the foot, moving tendons and other structures out of the way, removing the medial eminence, stabilizing the joint with Kirschner wire, and closing the patient up. This is procedure is best described by code 28292, and is accurately depicted in the accompanying diagram.

Respiratory, Cardiovascular, Hemic and Lymphatic, Mediastinum, and Diaphragm

81. **B** – For this question, look at the operative note for an explanation of what is being done, then look at each answer and dissect the codes. The operative note describes two coronary artery bypass grafts. One graft is a vein and the other is an artery. The second paragraph describes how the patient was opened up, the dissection performed to reach the heart and the harvesting of a mammary artery to be grafted to the heart. The third paragraph describes the harvesting of a femoral popliteal vein that will be used for a graft on the heart. The fourth paragraph describes sewing the artery and vein to the existing heart vessels prior to cutting the damaged portion out. The fifth paragraph describes the patient being placed on a machine that will breathe and beat his heart for him (cardiopulmonary bypass). Once this is done the surgeon cuts out the damaged heart vessels, and the ends of the new vessels are sewn to the exposed ends (anastomosis) of the remaining heart vessels. A chest tube is placed

for fluid drainage during recovery. Paragraph six describes the patient being closed up and sent to recovery. In this scenario, the opening and closure of the patient is part of the main procedure and should not be reported separately. Anastomosis is part of vessel grafting and is also bundled into the main procedure code. Cardiopulmonary bypass is considered an integral part of open heart surgery and should not be coded separately. Placement of a chest tube is only billed when it is not part of a larger procedure. Since a larger procedure was performed (CABG), the chest tube will not be coded here. Vessel harvesting may or may not be coded in addition to the primary codes depending in the type of vessel being harvested and the primary procedure's coding guidelines.

Option A: Code 35600 correctly describes the harvesting of an upper extremity artery that will be used as a graft for the heart; however, in this scenario, the mammary artery was harvested; according to the CABG coding guidelines (above codes 33510, 33517 and 33533), the procurement of any artery (except from the arm) is already included in the graft codes and should not be reported separately. This means that code 35600 cannot be used here. Code 35572 describes the harvesting of a femoralpopliteal vein. The same CABG coding guidelines tell us that a harvested vein is included in the grafting codes and should not be coded separately unless it is a femoralpopliteal vein. Since the vein that was harvested was a femoral popliteal vein, we are directed to use the additional code 35572. Code 33533 is also the correct code and accurately describes a single artery bypass done on a heart vessel (in this case the artery is the mammary and the heart vessel is the descending aorta). Code 33517 is correct because it describes a single vein being grafted when an artery is also being grafted during the same operation. Code 32551 correctly describes the placement of the chest tube; however, the code should not be used because the placement of a chest tube is included in a CABG. This is why there is a notation beneath code 32551 that says: "separate procedure." Code 36825 describes a procedure that joins two vessels (that are not on the heart) by a method other than anastomosis. This procedure was not performed in this scenario and should not be coded. Code 33926 describes cardiopulmonary bypass being used during the repair of an artery that links the lungs and heart - the pulmonary artery - (see code 33925 for the common descriptor) this was not performed here and should not be coded.

Option B: Code 33533 is correct for a single artery graft to the heart. Code 33517 is an add-on code for 33533 and accurately describes a single vein graft to a heart vessel when an artery graft is also performed. According to the CABG coding guidelines code 35572 should be used for femoral-popliteal vein harvesting. The procurement of the mammary artery, anasto-mosis, cardiopulmonary bypass and chest tube placement are all bundled with the CABG codes and should not be coded separately.

Option C: Code 33510 describes a vein being grafted to a heart vessel when only veins are being used. Since an artery and a vein were both graft-ed we would use code 33517 instead. Codes 33533 and 35572 were al-ready established as correct (see description under option A rational). Code 32551 (chest tube) is included in the CABG grafting procedures and should not be coded separately. Code 36821 describes anastomosis performed on vessels outside the heart for dialysis purposes, which was not performed here and should not be coded.

Option D: Code 33510 is the only incorrect code for this option. Code 33510 describes a vein being grafted to a heart vessel when only veins are being used. Since an artery and a vein were both grafted we would use code 33517 in addition to the artery code 33533 instead of code 33510.

82. **D** – Option A and C share the same description and provide different age brackets; options B and D also share the same description and provide dif-ferent age brackets. Option A and B are both for children five years and under. Since this patient is 50, we can eliminate options A and B. The difference between the remaining options (C and D) is the description "tunneled" catheter verses a "non-tunneled" catheter. A tunneled catheter enters the body, tunnels under the skin, and exits the body in a different location. A non-tunneled catheter enters the body and resides in the point of entry. This scenario describes the catheter entering and residing in/near the point of entery (subclavian). Most CPT books provide diagrams of these procedures above or below the corresponding codes and include a short description of the process. The diagram for code 36556 specifically states "the catheter tip must reside in the subclavian, innominate, or other iliac veins…"

83. **A** – The right lung has three lobes. When two lobes are removed, it is called a bilobectomy. When the entire lung is removed, it is called a total pneumonectomy. The left lung has only two lobes (so the heart has room to expand). When one lobe of the left lung is removed it is called a lobectomy and when two lobes are removed it is called a total pneumonectomy (because the entire lung is being removed). Because our question describes the left lung, code 32482 is incorrect. Code 32482 describes a bilobectomy, but in the case of the left lung, that would be the entire lung (total pneumonectomy). A pleaurectomy is the removal if the pleaura, not the lung or its lobes (32310). In this scenario a total pneumonectomy was performed, and it was in an open fashion (not laparoscopically - 32663).

84. **A** – In this example, the surgeon uses a scope to take two biopsies of tissue from a mediastinal mass. Since a scope was used, we can eliminate options C and D. Code 39000 (option C) describes an open procedure, while Code 32405 (option D) describes a procedure using a percutaneous needle. The difference between the remaining options, A and B, is the approach used. Code 32606 (option B) describes a thoracoscopy of the mediastinal space, and approaches through the chest wall, where the scope is maneuvered from the thorax into the mediastinal space. Code 39401 (option A) describes a mediastinoscopy, in which the surgeon makes an incision under the sternal notch at the base of the throat and the scope is maneuvered directly into the mediastinum, where a biopsy of a mediastinal mass is taken.

85. **C** – The notations below some of these codes will determine the best option here. Code 31237 states beside it "separate procedure," which means, if it was performed at the same time as another procedure, it must be bundled into the primary procedure rather than coded separately. Option(s) A and B can be eliminated because code 31237 is listed. Option B can also be eliminated because of code 31201, which describes an open ethmoidectomy, while this procedure was performed endoscopically. In option(s) C and D, code 31255 is correct, because it accurately describes an anterior and posterior removal of the ethmoid sinuses. Code 31295 (option D) was also performed and correctly coded; however, beneath the code, there is a notation stating that it should not be used in conjunction with code 31267, which is one of the correct codes in the answer. Code 31267 describes the nasal polyp removal; since we know that it cannot be used in conjunction with code 31295, option C is correct. Option C can also be deduced from reading the multiple notations beneath code 31256. The third notation states "for anterior and posterior ethmoidectomy (APE), and frontal sinus exploration, with or without polyp(s) removal, use 31255 and 31276."

86. **D** – In this question, the surgeon placed a permanent dual chamber pacemaker. Code 33240 (option A) describes an implantable defibrillator instead of a pacemaker. This eliminates option A. Option B has the correct code (33208) to describe the pacemaker placement with leads in both the atrial and ventricular chambers. Codes 33225 and 33202 are incorrect, though, because, according to the pacemaker coding guidelines found above code 33202 and the notations below code 33208, transvenous placement of electrodes is included in code 33208. Codes 33225 and 33202 should only be used when additional electrodes are placed. Code 33213 (option C) describes only the battery portion of the unit being placed. The notation below this code states that, if electrodes are coded, to use 33202 or 33203 (not code 33217, as given in option C). Option D accurately describes the placement of both the pacemaker generator and the two transvenous electrodes.

87. **B** – According to the endoscopy coding guidelines (found above code 31231), "A surgical sinus endoscopy includes a sinusotomy (when appropriate) and diagnostic endoscopy."

88. **C** – Code 36217 in options A and B describes the selective catheter placement to the third order, but in the wrong vascular family (36217 is for thoracic or brachiocephalic). The correct family is the "lower extremity," where the femoral artery is located. This eliminates options A and B. Code 36245 includes the common descriptor belonging to code 36247, and includes the correct "lower extremity" vascular family. Options C and D provide the correct catheterization, code but provide different ultrasound codes. Since the ultrasound was provided for the initial noncoronary vessel, and two additional noncoronary vessels (to get to the third order), code 37252 for the initial vessel and 37253 X2 for the second and third orders. These codes provide radiological supervision and interpretation.

89. **A** – The "indirect" view refers to looking at the larynx in an indirect fashion, such as a reflection. A "direct" view refers to looking directly at the larynx.

90. **D** – Code 38308 describes surgery performed on a lymphatic channel instead of a lymph node, so this code is incorrect. Here, the surgeon performed a biopsy of a lymphnode in the armpit (axillia). Code 38500 describes a biopsy, but is for a superficial one. The procedure describes dissection through the fascia (this covers the muscle), and the full excision of the entire lymphnode (which was then sent to pathology). Code 38510 has the correct common descriptor, which begins at code 38500 and reads "Biopsy or excision of lymphnode(s);". The unique descriptor of this code describes the location being on the neck instead of the axillia, so this code is also incorrect. Code 38525 accurately describes the biopsy/excision of the deep axillary nodes.

Digestive

91. **D** – The term esophagogastroduodenoscopy (abbreviated EGD) describes the viewing of the esophagus (esophago), the stomach (gastro), and the duodenum (duodeno), with a camera/scope (oscopy). Option A describes an esophagoscopy, which is a scope performed with a biopsy, but does not move farther than the esophagus. Option B describes an exavetmination of the upper GI, but does not describe the tissue sampling. Option C correctly describes an EDG, but a tissue sample is not the same as obtaining cells through brushing or washing. Since the physician actually took a sample, this code is also incorrect. Option D, code 43239, uses the same common descriptor in code 43235, but the unique descriptor (beside code 43239) correctly describes the tissue biopsy. There may also be a diagram of code 43235, which describes a scope going through the esophagus, stomach and to the duodenum. If so, the diagram may also help to narrow the options to C and D.

92. **C** – Endoscopy coding guidelines (above code 45300) state that a sigmoidoscopy is an endoscopy that advances to the descending colon, but no farther. A colonoscopy is an endoscopy that advances past the splenic flexure, into the cecum, and may go as far as the terminal ileum. The physician had planned to advance into the cecum, which means he was going to perform a colonoscopy, but he chose not to perform the entire colonoscopy due to unforeseen circumstances (fecal impaction). According to "coding tip" coding guidelines (above 45378 in the AMA Professional Edition), you should still code for the colonoscopy, and add modifier 53 to indicate that the entire procedure was not completed. This means that code 45378 with a 53 modifier is correct.

93. **A** – The operative note describes the open repair of a unilateral inguinal hernia with mesh placement (Marlex patch). Option A (code 49505) accurately describes the repair of a unilateral inguinal hernia (open), and includes the mesh placement - see hernia coding guidelines above code 49491. The fourth paragraph states "With the exception of the incisional hernia repairs (49560-49566), the use of mesh or other prostheses is not separately reported." Beneath code 49507, there is a notation stating that, if a simple orchiectomy (removal of a testicle) is also performed during the hernia repair, codes 49505 and/or 49507 should be used in conjunction with code

54520. In this scenario, however, an orchiectomy was not performed, so using codes 49505 or 49507 with code 54520 would be incorrect. This eliminates options B and D. Code 49568 describes the use of mesh during the repair of an incisional or venteral hernia only (this hernia was inguinal), and beneath this code is a list of the CPT codes it should be used in conjunction with. Code 49505 is not included in that list. Remember also the hernia coding guidelines (above code 49491) state that "with the exception of the incisional hernia repairs (codes 49560- 49566) the use of mesh or other prostheses in not separately reported."

94. **A** - This information can be found above code 40800 under the heading "Vestibule of Mouth." When looking up the term "vestibule" in the index you are told to see "mouth, vestibule of." Looking up this term should lead you near code 40800, where you will find the description of a vestibule (above the code).

95. **A** – The digestive system is made up of two portions: the alimentary canal and the accessory organs. The alimentary canal starts at the mouth and ends at the anus; the alimentary canal is what food passes through during the digestive process. Parts of the alimentary canal include the mouth, esophagus, stomach, and intestines. Accessory organs are organs that aid in digestion but do not come in direct contact with the food. Accessory organs include the gallbladder, liver, and pancreas. This information is not listed in the CPT book. Since the AAPC allows notations to be made in your books, it is a good idea to make a notation of this beside your digestive system diagram found within the Table of Contents for the Digestive System.

96. **C** - Codes 42826, 42831 and 42836 are all used to describe a tonsillectomy, or an adenoidectomy. Code 42821 is needed when the two operations are performed together, since items such as anesthesia, opening the patient and closing the patient can be bundled with the surgery codes. This eliminates options A and B. Code 42821 also does not need modifier 50 appended, since the code is used for total tonsillectomies and total adenoidectomies, rather than unilateral surgeries. ICD-10-CM code J03.90 correctly describes acute tonsillitis, which is an inflammation and differs from an abscess, which uses code J36, Peritonsillar abscess. Code J35.0 is incorrect because it has a fifth digit available, which was not used. Coding guidelines dictate that, if a fifth digit is available, it must be used. Code J35.03, Chronic tonsillitis and adenoiditis, is the correct answer.

97. A - The operative note describes an endoscopic percutaneous gastrostomy tube placement. Code 43246 describes this correctly (see code 43235 for the common descriptor). Modifier 62 is needed, because Dr. Smith performed only the tube placement. If he were to charge code 43246 with no modifier, he would be reimbursed for the EOG as well. Dr. Brown performed the EOG portion of this code, so he would also charge code 43246-62. This way each physician is reimbursed half. Code 49440 describes a non-endoscopic gastostomy tube placement. Code 43752 is also a non-endoscopic procedure. Code 43653 is a laparoscopic procedure, which means that an incision was created for the camera to enter the body, rather than an endoscopic procedure, which enters the body through an existing opening (e.g. mouth).

98. C - Code 43756 is not used for evacuation of stomach contents, but for things like bile studies. The duodenum is also where the stomach and small intestine connect, which was not mentioned in this scenario. Code 43752 describes the placement of a permanent tube meant for introducing nutrients or medication into the body, not for evacuation. Code 43753 is the correct code. Gastric intubation is the introduction of a tube into the stomach, and aspiration is synonymous with evacuation. Some CPT books (like the AMA's professional edition) have an added diagram of this code and a detailed description that includes key terms like "large-bore gastric lavage tube" and "evacuation of stomach contents". It also includes examples in which this code would be used, including poisonings. Option D describes a gastric intubation as well, which was performed here, but this code it is only performed for diagnostic purposes, not to correct a known problem (which would be therapeutic).

99. **B** – Endoscopies - not laparoscopies - performed in the digestive chapter run between codes 43180-43278; 44360-44408; 45300-45398; 46600-46615 and 47550-47556. There is a convention to the right of these codes that looks like a target, and they are there to indicate that moderate sedation is already included in that particular CPT code, and therefore cannot be coded separately. The definition to this convention is found in the front of the CPT book (Introduction, page xii in the AMA's Professional Edition), or at the bottom of every page in the CPT book. While the majority of the codes have this convention beside them, there are some which do not (45300; 45330; 45331; 46600-46615; 47550-47556). All codes that include moderate sedation are also listed in the back of the CPT book, in Appendix G. By referencing Appendix G, you will see that codes 45300; 45330; 45331; 46600-46615 and 47550-47556 are not listed as including moderate sedation
.

100. **A** – According to the Bariatric surgery coding guidelines above code 43770, a lap band adjustment consists of changing the restrictive band's diameter by means of injection or aspiration of fluid through a subcutaneous port. Because this description is under the laparoscopic heading, the procedure code should also be under the laparoscopic heading. Option B (43886) is an open procedure requiring sedation and an incision. The code's description also describes a revision to the actual port, not the lap band. Option C (43842) is an open procedure as well, which would require the patient to be in an operating room. This code describes the placement of a restrictive device, not the revision of one that is already in place. Option D (43848) is an open procedure code, and describes the revision of the restrictive procedure, not the revision of a restrictive device. Code 43771 in option A correctly describes a laparoscopic procedure (through an existing port) for the revision of an already placed restrictive device.

Urinary, Male Genital, and Female Genital Systems, and Maternity Care and Delivery

101. **D** – This question describes a patient with renal calculi (kidney stone), and a procedure that breaks the stone into smaller pieces (lithotripsy). The term "lith" means stone and the term "trip" means to break. Code 50590 describes the use of a lithotripsy wave machine (C-Arm image intensifier) to send shock waves from the outside of the body (extracorpeal). This code may also have a diagram describing lithotripsy in more detail. Radiology codes, such as 74425 and 76770, were not utilized here. Code 50081 describes a percutaneous procedure that enters the kidney from the outside (likely using a needle), and retrieves the stone without destroying it. Codes 50060 and 50130 both describe open procedures; the suffix –otomy means to cut into, so the terms nephrolithotomy and pyelolithotomy both involve cutting into the kidney (nephro and pyelo both mean kidney) to remove a stone (lith). Since neither an open procedure, and no incisions were made, these codes are also incorrect.

102. **B** – Code 57155 describes the placement of small radioactive elements, which are left in the patient for the duration of treatment prescribed, and later removed. Code 57156 describes the insertion of a vaginal radiation afterloading apparatus for clinical brachytherapy. This code should be used for the placement of vaginal cylinder rods, or similar afterloading devices. This procedure is typically performed in a post-hysterectomy patient. An "afterloading apparatus" is described as a technique in which the radioactivity is loaded after proper placement of the apparatus has been confirmed. The rods (or afterloading device) should have an access port on the outside of the body, which can then be hooked up to an external machine capable of delivering either high dose or low dose rate brachytherapy. Although the patient recently had a hysterectomy, we are not told exactly how long ago, or by whom. Since we cannot assume anything, modifier 58 is not applied.

103. **D** – This scenario describes a vasectomy. Option A describes the "ligation" of the vas deferens, which is one form of vasectomy in which the vas deferens is tied off, or "strangulated," in order to block the exit of semen. This procedure does not require dissection or removal of the tube, as is described in this scenario. Option(s) B and C are used to describe a vasectomy reversal. As the two suffixes imply, -ostomy means to create

a permanent opening (e.g. opening a ligated vas deferns), and -orraphy means to repair. Depending on which version of the CPT book you own, you may be able to locate common terms like these in the front of the manual (e.g. AMA professional edition on page xiv). Code 55250 in option D accurately describes the performance of a vasectomy, unilateral or bilateral.

104. B - Option A is a laparoscopic procedure, and in this scenario, an open procedure was performed. Option C describes a total nephrectomy (removal of the entire kidney), along with the removal of part of the uterus and a rib resection (removal of a portion or all of the rib). Here, only a portion of the kidney was removed, and there is no mention of the uterus or ribs being removed (only dissected through). Code 50290 in option D describes the removal of a perinephric cyst, which is an accumulation of fluid in a cyst-like mass between the kidney and surrounding capsule. There is no mention of a perinephric cyst, so this is also incorrect. In this scenario a portion of the kidney containing the tumor was removed in an open fashion. The term nephro- means kidney and the suffix -ectomy means to remove. This is accurately described by code 50240, Nephrectomy, partial. Common prefixes, Root Words, and Suffixes may be located in the beginning of your CPT book.

105. B - For twin gestations, report the deliveries separately with no modifier on the first infant and modifier 51 on the second infant. If antepartum and postpartum care is provided, report the obstetric services for the first infant and report the appropriate delivery-only code for the second infant using modifier 51. Modifier 51 indicates multiple procedures are being billed and this is not the primary procedure. This means that code 59618, which describes a caesarean delivery after a previous caesarean delivery, a vaginal birth attempt (according to the coding guidelines above code 59610) and includes antepartum and postpartum care, is correct for the first infant. Code 59620-51 is correct for the second infant. In answer D, modifier 22 on the single code 59618 is not correct because a single procedure requiring more work was not performed. With the CPT codes alone, the answer is determined to be B. Alternatively, using the ICD codes, note that code Z38.4, Twin liveborn infant, born outside of hospital, is incorrect. This eliminates answers A and D. To find all the ICD-10-CM codes, look up Exhaustion, maternal, complicating delivery which indicates O75.81. Also, look up Pregnancy, twin monochorionic/ monoamniotic (one placenta, one amniotic sac) in the ICD-10-CM Index, which indicates O30.01-. The full code is O30.013, used for the third trimester. Look up Pregnancy, complicated by preterm labor, third trimester, with third trimester, preterm delivery in the index to find code O60.14. For a multiple gestation, the fetuses are numbered in utero. It was unspecified which fetus was causing the preterm labor, so the 7th digit is 0, making the full code is O60.14XO. Code O60.14XO is in answer B but not C, so B is indeed the correct answer. Look up Delivery, failed, attempted vaginal birth after previous caesarean delivery in the ICD-10-CM Index, which points to O66.41. Look up Delivery, caesarean without indication, in the ICD-10-CM Index to find O82. There is a note to use additional code to indicate outcome of delivery, Z37.0. However, the Tabular indicates that the correct code is Z37.2 for Twins, both liveborn. Look up Pregnancy, weeks of gestation, 36 weeks, or Z3A.36.

106. **A** - According to the maternity care and delivery guidelines (prior to code 59000), in the middle of the third paragraph, "When reporting delivery only services (59409, 59514, 59612 and 59620), report inpatient post delivery management and discharge services using Evaluation and Management service codes.

107. **C** - PSA is an antigen tested in males to detect prostate cancer. Any reading over 10 is considered high. In this scenario, the patient is having a prostate biopsy performed to determine whether he has prostate cancer or benign prostate hypertrophy. Option A describes a needle or catheter being place by the transperineal approach, for the purpose of introducing small radioactive elements into the body to kill cancerous cells. Option B also describes a transperineal approach with the use of a needle for a prostate biopsy; however, it also describes a sterotactic template guided saturation sampling. A saturation biopsy is an alternative technique utilized by urologists to detect cancer in high risk patients by taking multiple samples (usually 30 or more). This code also includes the imaging guidance so a 70000 code (like 76942) should not be coded in addition to it. Code 55705 in option D is used to describe a biopsy taken by an open procedure. This would include an incision and repair. Code 55700 accurately describes a prostate biopsy, by needle or punch, by any approach (including retroperineal). Notations beneath this code also direct you to code 76942 for ultrasonic guidance if performed.

108. A - A hydrocele is a pathological fluid filled sack within the scrotum. This question describes a bilateral hydrocelectomy of the tunic vaginalis. What makes this question difficult is that medicinally a hydrocelectomy and a hydrocele repair are sometimes used synonymously. Code 54861 in option B describes a procedure removing both of the Epididymis tubes, and has no mention of a hydrocele. This rules out option B. Code 55000-50 in option C describes a procedure performed on both tunic vaginalis, but it is a puncture aspiration (a hole punched with a needle to drain the fluid), so this can be ruled out as well, since our physician performed an incision and dissection. Choosing between code 55060 in option D and code 55041 in option A comes down to the type of procedure and its

details. Code 55060 is a "bottle" type procedure, also known as "Andrews Procedure." This procedure requires a 2-3 cm incision in the hydrocele sack near the superior portion (or top), and requires tacking the cut edges around the cord structures, leaving the everted sac open. When choosing between these two codes, note the heading that each code is under. Code 55041 is under the "Excision" heading, and code 55060 is under the "Repair" heading. In a hydrocele excision (code 55041), the majority of the sac is removed. In a hydrocele repair (code 55060), the sac is cut open and the edges are tacked back. The procedure is also described as a "hydrocelectomy," and the suffix – ectomy means to remove (similar to the excision).

109. B – Code 51797 should not be used without its primary code. Beneath code 51797, it states that this code should be used in addition to either code 51728 or 51729. Since options A and C utilize code 51797 without its primary code, both are incorrect. Code 51729 utilizes the common descriptor next to code 51726, but also has its own unique descriptor "with voiding pressure studies," making its full description "Complex cystometrogram (e.g. Calibrated electronic equipment); with voiding pressure studies." Code 51797 is an add-on code describing the "intra-abdominal" portion, and it is noted that this code should be used in addition to code 51729. This means that the codes in options B and C are correct. According to the Urodynamics coding guidelines (above code 51725), if the physician did not provide the equipment and is simply operating it and interpreting the report, modifier 26 should be added to these codes. Since the physician here is utilizing hospital equipment rather than his own, modifier 26 is should be added.

110. **C** – Code 58976 describes the transfer of an already fertilized egg within the fallopian tube. In this scenario, the eggs are unfertilized and being harvested from the ovarian follicles, rather than transferred. Code 58672 is a laparoscopic procedure (instead of a percutaneous procedure), and describes the *repair* of a fimbio. Code 58970 correctly describes the harvesting of the unfertilized eggs from the ovarian follicle with an ultrasonic guided needle. Beneath this code there is a notation stating that code 76948 is to be used for radiological supervision and interpretation. Code 58940 is used to describe the removal of one or both ovaries.

Endocrine, Nervous, Ocular, and Auditory Systems

111. B – To find the answer for this question, use the anatomical diagrams in the auditory chapter. There are two diagrams in the auditory chapter that have pictures of the ossicles. One diagram depicts a tympanoplasy (codes 69635 – 69646), and the other diagram depicts a tympanostomy (codes 69433-69436). Although the ossicles are not labeled individually, they are labeled "Ossicles." Using the picture of the three ossicles, you look at a second diagram of the ear located in the the Auditory System Table of Contents (prior to code 69000). The same picture of the three ossicles is shown, but this time they are labeled individually as the Incus, Malleus, and Stapes. Writing the terms hammer, anvil, and stirrup beneath these three diagrams may be useful when taking the CPC Exam (this is an AAPC approved notation; these diagrams are in the AMA's Professional CPT Edition, 2016).

112. C – Code 62160 in options A and D describes the use of a neuroendoscope, which is not mentioned in this scenario, so these options are incorrect. Options B and C are very similar, except that code 61210 describes a burr hole and code 61107 describes a twist drill hole. The difference is that a burr hole is created with an electronic drill and a special bit, while the twist drill is a manually operated hand tool. Code 61107 also describes a puncture method, which is performed with a needle, rather than an incision made with a scalpel.

113. A – Code 63040 is for a laminectomy (removal of the lamina), a partial facetectomy (removal of the facet) and nerve decompression (with or without removal of a herniated disc). Focus on the key passages in this question: "the ligamentum flavum, lamina and fragments of a ruptured C3-C4 intervertebral disc were all removed," "the surgeon removed a portion of the facet" and "to relieve the compressed nerve." Code 63075 in option B describes an anterior approach (from the front of the body). Since this scenario describes a posterior approach (from the back of the body), this code can be eliminated. Code 63075 also describes the removal of a herniated disc, which would require the sternocleoidmastoid muscle and carotid artery be retracted, the removal of the disc and a T shaped graft from the ilium. These things were not described in this scenario though. Code 63081 describes a vertebral corpectomy, which is the removal (-ectomy) of the vertebral corpus. A corpectomy would require the surgeon to incise the dura, locate denated ligaments and section them. Closure could either include or not include a graft.

Code 63170 (option D) describes a laminectomy with a myelotomy (myle- meaning muscle and -otomy meaning to cut into). This procedure includes the laminectomy described in this scenario, but the surgeon would incise the dura and the outer white matter of the spinal cord as well, which was not performed.

114 **C** – Keratoplasty means to repair the cornea (kerato means cornea and -plasty means repair). A keratoplasty of the anterior lamellar is a surgical procedure that removes the corneal stroma down the descemet's membrane. This is a partial thickness graft that preserves the two innermost layers of the cornea. Keratomileusis (kerato means cornea and mieusis means to carve or shape) is a type of lasik eye surgery. Here, the ophthalmologist creates a flap of corneal tissue, then uses a laser to remold the original cornea, then the cornea flap is replaced. Keratophakia (kerato means cornea and phakia means lens) is the procedure described in this scenario (which uses a donor lens). Keratoprosthesis (kerato means cornea and prosthesis means an artificial substitute) is the replacement of the cornea with an artificial one that is bioengineered.

115. **C** – The endocrine system codes start with code 60000 and end with code 60699. The first heading in the endocrine chapter is "thyroid gland." Following the codes through the chapter, you come to code 60500, and the next heading directly above the code, which reads: "Parathyroid, Thymus, Adrenal Glands, Pancreas and Carotid Body." The only organ not listed in the endocrine chapter is the Lymph nodes, which are part of the hemic-lymphatic system, located at the end of the 30000 codes.

116 **C** – The coding guidelines above code 69990 (operating microscope) state that this code should not be coded with codes from code range 65091 to 68850. Since both code 67107 and 67101 are within that code range, the operating microscope should not be coded with them.

This eliminates option(s) B and D. Code 67101 and code 67107 differ little, but code 67107 includes the terms "sclera buckling" and "including, when performed, implant." The band placed around the eye causes sclera buckling and, in this scenario, there was not an implant. Code 67107 is the more specific code for the scenario described. This code is also explained further with diagrams in some CPT books..

117. **C** – The neurosurgeon performed a crainiotomy (cut into the skull; craini- means head, and -otomy means to cut into) and drained an intracerebellar hematoma (collection of blood). Code 61154 describes the burr hole accurately, but not a craniotomy. It also describes the evacuation of the hematoma correctly, but it is missing the location (intracerebellum). This eliminates options A and D. Code 61315 correctly describes the scenario "Craniectomy or crainiotomy for evacuation of hematoma, infratentorial; intracerebellar." Although the neurosurgeon did create a burr hole during the procedure, notations beneath code 61253 state "if burr- holes or trephine are followed by a crainiotomy at the same operative ses-sion, use 61304-61321; do not use 61250 or 61253."

118. **D** – The primary difference in these codes is the specific nerve being de-compressed. Code 64702 describes a nerve decompression for a finger or toe. Code 64704 is also a nerve decompression, but for a hand or foot. Code 64719 is the code used for a nerve decompression of the ulnar nerve of the wrist. Code 64721, which is described in this scenario, is the nerve decompression of the median nerve (e.g. carpal tunnel surgery).

119. **B** – The procedure performed here is a repair to a fistula in the round window. Code(s) 69666 and 69667 accurately describe this procedure, but code 69666 is performed on the oval window, while code 69667 is performed on the round window. Options A and C are ruled out, because they utilize the oval window code instead of the round window code. There are no notations beneath code 69667 excluding modifier 50, and coding guidelines say that if a procedure is not noted as a bilateral operation (or is not specified in the guidelines), then it is assumed to be unilateral. Since code 69667 is not noted as being bilateral, we must assume that it is unilateral. Since the surgeon performed this procedure on both ears, modifier 50 is correct. Code 69990 has a list of CPT codes it cannot be coded with (see Operating Microscope Coding Guidelines above code 69990). However, code 69667 is not one of them, so coding 69990 in addition to code 69667 is correct.

120. **B** – Code 60512 is an add-on code, and beneath it is a list of codes it can be "added onto." This list includes code 60260 (option A), code 60240 which is a total thyroidectomy (Option C) and code 60500 (Option C). Add-on codes are always added onto a primary procedure code and are never to be used as a primary code or as a single code (see General Coding Guidelines, Add-on Codes, pg. xvi, AMA Professional Edition 2016).

Integumentary

121. **C** – The full CPT code has two components: technical and professional. If the physician did not perform both components, he cannot be reimbursed for both. The TC modifier is used to depict the technical component, which is what the radiologist often utilizes. Modifier 26 is the professional component, which is what the physician should append to his CPT code. Modifier 52 is used when a physician must terminate a procedure or attempts an entire procedure but has unsuccessful results. A full description of modifiers 26 and 52 can be found in appendix A. Modifier TC is an HCPCS modifier and should be referenced in the HCPCS book.

122. **A** – According to the chart provided above code 74176, the guidelines above it and the notation beneath code 74178, code 74178 is a standalone code. The guidelines state: "do not report more than one CT of the abdomen or CT of the pelvis for any single session." Using the chart, the last box across the top: *74170 CT of the Abdomen without contrast followed by with contrast (WO//W Contrast)*, and the top box on the side *72192, CT of the Pelvis without contrast (WO Contrast)* should be selected. Following both selections to the point where they intersect, you end up in the last box at the first (non-bold) column, containing code 74178. Notations beneath this code state: "Do not report 74176 – 74178 in conjunction with 72192 – 72194, 74150 – 74170."

123. **C** – The radiologist took three views of the patient's facial bones: the Water's view (oblique anterior-posterior), anterior-posterior view and lateral view. Code 70100 is a view of the mandible only, which is located in the jaw. Code 70120 describes three views of the mastoid, which is located near the ear, and attached to the temporal bone. Code 70150 accurately describes three views taken of unspecified facial bones. Code 70250 describes skull bones, not facial bones, being viewed.

124. **A** – The "Aorta and Arteries" coding guidelines (above code 75600) state that a diagnostic angiography may be reported with an interventional procedure when performed together under specific circumstances. One such circumstance is when a prior report is recorded in the medical

record, but states there is inadequate visualization of the anatomy. These guidelines also state modifier 59 needs to be appended to the diagnostic radiological supervision and interpretation. To find this information, use the alphabetic index and look up the term "angiography." The index will direct you to "see aortography." Looking up the term "Aorta, aortography" leads you to code 75600, and the guidelines above it.

125. **B** – For the bone biopsy, code 20225 accurately describes a percutaneous deep bone biopsy. Code 20245 describes the same thing, only it is an open instead of a percutaneous (requiring an incision instead of a needle) procedure. Code 38221 is a biopsy of the bone marrow, not the actual bone. Beneath code 20225, the notations say to use either code 77002, 77012 or 77021 for radiological supervision and interpretation. Code 77012 accurately depicts the CAT scan (computed tomography). Code 76998 describes the use of an ultrasound instead of a CAT scan and code 73700 is used when a diagnostic CAT scan is being taken, not a procedural one.

126. **C** – High dose radiation (HDR) brachytherapy, or internal radiation, delivers radiation directly to the tumor by placing high-dose radioactive materials inside the cancerous area and then removing them, usually after a short period of time. HDR brachytherapy differs from intracavitary brachytherapy, which places lower dosed radioactive materials in the cancerous area for longer periods of time. The unit that holds the radioactive sources is called an afterloader and the materials are delivered to the tumor through channels, usually a catheter. Codes for intracavitary brachytherapy are not determined by the number of channels used, but the number of radioactive sources delivered (see coding guidelines above code 77750). Interstitial radiation is similar to intracavitary radiation except that instead of placing the radioactive elements in a body cavity, they are placed in body tissue. Code 77762 (A) describes intracavitary radiation, but not the high dose radiation, so it is incorrect. Code 77790 (B) is used when charging for the handling of the radioactive elements and equipment before and after the procedure. Code 77771 (C), accurately describes the delivery of high-dose radiation using a remote afterloading device with 2-12 channels; in this scenario, three channels were used. Code 77770 (D) is high-dose radiation using a remote afterloading device, but only for one channel (rather than than three), so it is incorrect.

127. **A** – There is little difference between codes 78451 and 78453. Code 78451 is done by SPECT, and includes attenuation correction, while code 78453 is a planar type image. In this scenario, code 78451 is correct. This rules out option(s) B and D. According to the Radiology Cardiovascular System coding guidelines above code 78414, when a myocardial perfusion study using codes 78451-78454 or 78472-78492 is performed in conjunction with a stress test, the stress test should be coded in addition to the study using codes 93015-93018. Here, code 93016 is correct because the physician did not provide the interpretation and report (the cardiologist did).

128. **C** – The fluid at the back of the fetuses' neck is also known as the nuchal fold, or nuchal translucency. When this is too thick, it is an indication that the fetus may have Down syndrome. Option A describes an ultrasound for both the fetuses and the mother. In this scenario, only the fetuses are being evaluated, so this eliminates option A. Option B also includes a maternal evaluation, so this too is incorrect. Option C correctly describes the first trimester, fetus evaluation only, is specific to the nuchal translucency and includes a transabdominal approach. Add-on code 76814 is also correct when reporting multiple gestations; according to notations beneath code 76814, this code should be used in conjunction with code 76813 when reporting multiple gestations. Option D describes a reevaluation to confirm a prior finding. In this scenario, there is no mention of a prior screening.

129. **A**– Code 3598 accurately describes the injection of a contrast material (radiopaque iodine) into a central venous access device (Hickman's catheter). This code also includes the fluoroscopic imaging and report. According to the notations beneath code 36598, it is not to be coded in conjunction with code 76000, so option C is incorrect. These notations state that, if you are looking to code complete diagnostic studies, see 75820, 75825 and 75827. It does not, however, say you must use them in addition to this code. Radiology "Vein and Lymphatic" coding guidelines above code 75801 State: "Diagnostic venography is performed at the same time as an interventional procedure it is NOT separately reportable if it is specifically included in the interventional code descriptor." In this scenario, there is not clear indication that a full vein study was performed, only a CVAD check. Since code 36598 includes the fluoroscopic imaging and report there is nothing else to report.

130. **A** – The radiology coding guidelines prior to code 70010 in the last paragraph state that a signed written report is an integral part of the radiologic service or interpretation.

Pathology and Laboratory

131. **C** – When coding a panel, every test in that panel must be performed, or it cannot be coded. Every code listed in this scenario is listed beneath code 80053, except for the TSH, which is coded using code 84443. Code 80053 has an additional test for Albumin listed. Since an Albumin level was not ordered, we cannot use code 80053, even with a 52 modifier. This eliminates option A. Option B lists total calcium levels being ordered instead of ionized calcium levels, so this is incorrect. Option C is correct because every test listed beneath code 80047 was ordered. In addition to 80047, the lab tests not listed are accurately coded individually. Option D seems like a good option because it accurately captures each test listed in this scenario. Code 80047 captures a larger number of tests, while still being correct, and utilizes fewer codes, making it the better option. When given a choice between a panel and listing each test individually, you should select the panel.

132. **A** – Only a gross examination was performed here. There is no mention of a microscopic examination, so even though an ovary is not specifically listed beneath code 88300, it is the only code that does not include the microscopic examination.

133. **B** – Appendix A has a full description of each modifier and how it should and should not be used. Modifier 99 should be used when a single CPT code has two or more modifiers appended to it. Modifier 99 could be used in place of the multiple modifiers, and the specific modifiers could then be listed elsewhere on a claim form. Modifier 76 is meant to be used on a service and/or procedure code, not laboratory codes. The use of modifier 76 eliminates option A. Modifier 91 is meant to be used with laboratory codes, and is used when a test is purposely run more than once on the same day. Modifier 91 should only be appended to the second test and beyond, but not to the first test performed (like in option C). Option B is correct because it lists each test once without a modifier and then the second and third time each of those tests were ran modifier 91 was appended, indicating that it was actually performed multiple times in one day. If option D were billed, the insurance company would pay each test only once and

then deny the second and third time the test was run as a "duplicate charge," because the 91 modifier was not appended to indicate they were not duplicates.

134. **B** – Code 81005 in option(s) A and D is used for an analysis of the urine for things like protein, glucose and bacteria. This is often performed using a dipstick, and may include a microscopic examination. This is not what is described in this scenario, so option(s) A and D are eliminated. Code 81025 accurately describes a urine test which provides a positive or negative result (in this case, pregnancy). Code(s) 84702 and 84703 are both used when testing for the growth hormone hCG. Code 84703 is a qualitative test that checks whether hCG is present or not. Code 84702 is a quantitative test, usually run to confirm a pregnancy, and provides a specific level of the hormone, such as 12500 mIU/ml.

135. **D** – The first drug test performed on the random urine sample tests for all four drugs and is considered a presumptive test, or a test that only gives a positive or negative result. All four of the drugs are in Drug Class List A. Code 80300 - for Drug screen, any number of drug classes from Drug Class List A using non-TLC procedures - is correct and we only code it once, since it covers any number of tests. Code 80301 is incorrect because the drug screen was not done by single drug class method. Code 80302, which is used for Class List B drugs, is incorrect. The correct codes for the barbiturates and opiates tests are 80345 and 80361, respectively.

136. C – CBC stands for complete blood count. Codes for a CBC are 85025 and 85027. These codes can be found by looking up "CBC" in the index and following the cross-reference. The codes' descriptions in the tabular index explain that a CBC includes Hgb (hemoglobin), Hct (hematocrit), RBC (red blood cell count), WBC (white blood cell count) and platelet count. Not included in a CBC is hCG (human chorionic gonadotropin), which is a human growth hormone that is elevated in pregnancy and often tested for to confirm the stage of pregnancy.

137. B – Code 89255 is used to describe a fertilized egg being prepared for implantation into a woman's uterus. Code 89258 is the code used when taking an embryo and preserving it by freezing (the medical prefix cryo- means cold). This is what the technician did in this scenario. Code 89268 describes the egg (oocyte) being fertilized with the sperm to form a zygote. And code 89342 is a code that is used when an embryo is already frozen and is simply being stored.

138. D – A glucose tolerance test (GTT) requires the patient to have blood drawn prior to the adminstration of glucose. He then receives glucose in some form and has blood drawn at intervals to determine how his body metabolizes the glucose. Code 82951 is the correct code for this test, and includes the pre-glucose blood draw, the glucose dose and the three blood draws following the ingestion. Code 82946 is also a tolerance test, but it is for glucagon, not glucose. Code 82950 is a glucose test that that is similar to the GTT, but does not require a blood draw prior to the glucose, and is usually checked only once, two hours after the glucose dose is received. According to appendix A, modifier 91 should not be used when a test is re-run due to a testing problem. Because the laboratory caused the issue, the patient's insurance should not be charged for two tests.

139. C - Code 80047 in options B and D has both carbon dioxide and sodium, but it contains ionized calcium, not total calcium. This eliminates options B and D. Option A has the individual codes for carbon dioxide, total calcium and sodium, but lists no panel codes. By default, option C is correct. Each of the codes listed in option C (80048, 80053 and 80069) are panel codes, and each one has all three of the elements listed: carbon dioxide, total calcium and sodium.

140. **A** – This is true of many tests, not just hCH. Generally, a qualitative test is a simple test that usually produces a positive or negative result. A quantitative test is usually a more sensitive method for testing or confirming a substance, and will provide results such as specific levels of the substance being tested for.

Medicine

141. B - First, look up laceration, arm (upper), which points to S41.11- with the full code being S41.112A, to indicate the left side, initial encounter. Next, look up Laceration, cheek, right in the ICD-10-CM Index, which will indicate S01.41- with the full code being S01.411A to indicate the right side, initial encounter. Finally, look up Exposure, rabies to find Z20.3. The laceration coding guidelines above code 12001 specify that the lengths of lacerations located in the same anatomical grouping, and requiring the same depth or repair, may be added together for a single code selection. Since the two lacerations were both on the arm, and both required a layered repair, you should add their lengths (1 cm + 4 cm = 5 cm), so 12032 is the correct code. The single laceration on the face was a simple repair, which is found in the code range 12011 – 12018; the correct code here is 12013 (2.6 – 5.0 cm). Since this is a secondary procedure, append modifier 51. Moving to the rabies injection, the applicable code here will be determined by the coding guidelines and the distinction between an immune globulin immunization and a toxoid vaccination. An immune globulin is defined as a substance that is administered in order to prevent an illness and provides passive immunization, and protects the body for a short period of time by introducing antibodies into the bloodstream which were obtained from another person's plasma. Conversely, a toxoid vaccination is the introduction of a dead virus into the bloodstream in order to stimulate the immune system to create its own antibodies, providing long-term protection. In this scenario, a toxoid vaccination was administered; code 96372 in option A is specific to SQ (subcutaneous) or IM (intramuscular) injections, but applies to therapeutic (curative), prophylactic (preventative) or diagnostic injections. The notation beneath this code specifies for vaccines/toxoids, see code 90460, 90461, 90471 or 90472. Guidelines for codes 90471 and 90472, located above code 90460, titled "immunization administration for vaccines and toxoids" state that codes 90471 (option C) and code 90472 are for individuals over the age of 18. Since this patient is 5, option C is incorrect. These guidelines specify that you used codes 90460 and 90461. The description for this code specifies the correct age range for this patient, includes the physician's counseling of the parents and describes a toxoid vaccine administration. The first sentence of these guidelines (above code 90460) instructs you to use you to use a code from the 90476 - 90749 range in addition to code 90460. So the additional code to describe the substance being injected is not code 90375, because a toxoid, rather than an immune globulin, was administered. Thus, we can eliminate options A and D. Code 90675 is within the specified code range (90476 – 90749), and describes an IM rabies vaccination. In the third paragraph of the Vaccine/Toxoid coding guidelines located about code 90476, it states that code 90675 is only for the substance, and that the administration code should come from code range 90460 – 90474, and that modifier 51 should NOT be appended to the substance code.

142. **A** - Since the physician did not perform the EKG, he cannot use code 93000, which includes this test. Options B and D can be eliminated. Normal saline was infused for 1 hour and 45 minutes, so codes 96360 and 96361 can be used by the supervising physician. According to the hydration coding guidelines above code 96360, this code may only be used for the initial hour, so add-on code 96361 must be used for each additional increment of time. A notation beneath the 96361 code states that it may be used for time increments of 30 minutes or greater if the total infusion time is at least 1 hour and 30 minutes. The CPT guidelines say that codes 96360 – 96361 may not be reported by physicians in a facility setting, but they can be used in this scenario, since this patient was treated on an outpatient basis, rather than an inpatient basis in a facility or hospital setting..

143. **D** - The "End-Stage Renal Disease Services" coding guidelines above code 90951 will determine the correct answer here. According to these guidelines, code 90960 is used when providing these services in an outpatient setting, such as a physician's office, but not for home dialysis. This eliminates option A. Code 90966 is for home dialysis and correctly describes the patient's age bracket (20 and older). However, according to the guidelines, these codes cannot be used for patients receiving services for less than a full month (30 days). This eliminates option B. According to the coding guidelines and the description of code 90970, this code should be reported for each day of service outside any inpatient setting. This leaves option D as the correct choice. The physician performed dialysis on the 15th – 18th (4 days), and then resumed dialysis on the 25th – 31st (7 days). For the month, the physician should charge 11 days.

144. **D** – The patient has an implantable cardioverter-defibrillator (ICD) that has implantable cardiovascular monitoring (ICM) functionalities. According to the ICM coding guidelines "when ICM functionality is included in an ICD device, the ICM data and the ICD heart rhythm data, such as sensing, pacing, and tachycardia detection therapy, are distinct and, therefore, the monitoring processes are distinct," and for that reason coded separately. Coding for the ICD includes 90 days of remote analysis and one face-to-face encounter for programming. Code 93295 is used once every 90 days for reporting remote analysis of an ICD and code 93283 is used to describe the in-person encounter for programming and adjustments made to the ICD. Codes for the ICM include 90 days of remote analysis. Although the physician also provided an in-person encounter for the ICM, the second paragraph of the coding guidelines state that "a physician may NOT report an in-person and remote interrogation device evaluation when they are performed during the same period." Instead, the guidelines instruct coders to bill for remote services only when both remote and in-person services are provided during the same time billing period. There are also notations beneath codes 93297 and 93290 stating that they should not be coded together. Code 93297 covers remote analysis of an ICM and is reported once every 30 days. The code would then be recorded as 93297 x3, since there are three periods of 30 days in 90 days equal three periods of 30 days each.

145. **B** – According to ophthalmology coding guidelines, comprehensive ophthalmological service includes the following: history; general medical observation; external examinations (lids, sclera, conjunctiva); ophthalmoscopic examinations (slit lamp/Goldman 3-mirror lens); gross visual fields and basic sensorimotor examinations (vertical prism bars, function of ocular motor system). Often included are cycloplegia (a drug used to dilate the pupils) and tonometry, a procedure used to measure fluid pressure inside the eye ("17 mm on each eye.") Diagnostic and treatment plans are always included (dx: cataracts and macular degeneration; tx: continued vitamins and surgery.) The coding guidelines state that "itemization of services, such as slit lamp examinations, keratometry, routine ophthalmoscopy, retinoscopy, tonometry, and motor evaluation is not applicable." Since this scenario meets all the requirements to code an established, comprehensive ophthalmological service, additional codes, such as 92060 and 92081, cannot be used because they are already bundled into service code 92014.

146. **A** – The rules regarding "separate procedures" and the 59 modifier are located under the second title in the medicine coding guidelines, "Separate Procedure." These rules apply to all CPT codes, not just those in the medicine chapter, and the stipulations are repeated in several other coding guidelines as well.

147. **B** – The simplest way to code this is to code for one day and then multiply that code by the number of visits for that month. The visits add up to 13 for this month, and there were four Fridays. When coding for a single day, you would use code 99601 as the initial peritoneal infusion code, and code 99602 for the additional hour. These codes would be used on all three days that the nurse visits and code 99509 would be added on to one day each week for the additional services performed on Fridays. Code 90966 is not correct because this code requires a full month of service. Code 99512 is also incorrect because this code is for hemodialysis, not peritoneal dialysis, and even has a notation beneath it instructing readers to use codes 99601 and 99602 when coding for home infusion of peritoneal dialysis. It would be incorrect to code one initial infusion code (99601) and the rest of the visits as code (99602 x25), because code 99601 states that it should be used "per visit." This means that code 99601 should be used for each individual date of service, with the add-on code 99602 for each date of service (99601 x13 and 99602 x13). For the four Fridays, code 99509 would be coded as 99509 x4.

148. **D** – Code 93923 describes a similar scenario, but includes additional studies. Three levels of plethymography volume are taken for code 93923, instead of the two levels in this procedure, and three or more oxygen tension measurements are taken with code 93923, instead of just two, so options A and B are wrong. Code 93922 accurately describes our scenario. The notation beneath code 93922 in the coding guidelines states that if a single extremity (instead of both) is being studied, modifier 52 must be added to the procedure code, which eliminates option C. The guidelines for this code may be found above code 93880, under the heading "Noninvasive Vascular Diagnostic Studies," in the fifth section which covers "Limited studies for lower extremity" and includes "ABI's (ankle/brachial indices) being taken at the posterior (back) and anterior (front) lower aspects of the tibial and tibial/dorsalis pedis arteries; Plethymography levels; Oxygen tension reading."

149. **B** – Code 91010 describes a manometric study, but it pertains to the esophagus, or throat, and gastroesophageal junction, which is where the stomach and esophagus meet. This eliminates answer choices A and D. Code 91020, (Gastric motility), is also a manometric study, and accurately describes this scenario. "Gastric" or "gastro" are synonymous for stomach and "motility" in this case is the ability to move food through the digestive tract. Code 91022 is incorrect because it describes the study of movement through the duodenum, which is the first portion of the small intestine, not from the stomach into the small intestine.

150. **A** – Coding conventions are listed to the left of each code. Each convention has its own meaning, which can be found with a short description at the bottom of each page. A full description can be found at the front of the CPT book. The coding convention that looks like a lightning bolt means "FDA approval pending." Codes 90666, 90667 and 90668 each have this convention listed beside them. Code 90664 does not have this coding convention listed beside it, so we know that it has FDA approval.

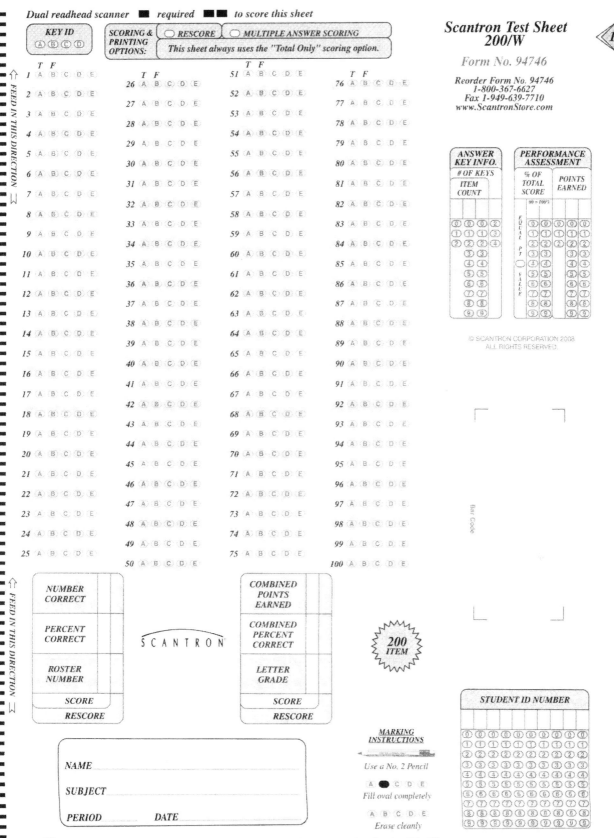

SCANTRON

	T F	A B C D E
101		A B C D E
102		A B C D E
103		A B C D E
104		A B C D E
105		A B C D E
106		A B C D E
107		A B C D E
108		A B C D E
109		A B C D E
110		A B C D E
111		A B C D E
112		A B C D E
113		A B C D E
114		A B C D E
115		A B C D E
116		A B C D E
117		A B C D E
118		A B C D E
119		A B C D E
120		A B C D E
121		A B C D E
122		A B C D E
123		A B C D E
124		A B C D E
125		A B C D E

T F
126 A B C D E
127 A B C D E
128 A B C D E
129 A B C D E
130 A B C D E
131 A B C D E
132 A B C D E
133 A B C D E
134 A B C D E
135 A B C D E
136 A B C D E
137 A B C D E
138 A B C D E
139 A B C D E
140 A B C D E
141 A B C D E
142 A B C D E
143 A B C D E
144 A B C D E
145 A B C D E
146 A B C D E
147 A B C D E
148 A B C D E
149 A B C D E
150 A B C D E

T F
151 A B C D E
152 A B C D E
153 A B C D E
154 A B C D E
155 A B C D E
156 A B C D E
157 A B C D E
158 A B C D E
159 A B C D E
160 A B C D E
161 A B C D E
162 A B C D E
163 A B C D E
164 A B C D E
165 A B C D E
166 A B C D E
167 A B C D E
168 A B C D E
169 A B C D E
170 A B C D E
171 A B C D E
172 A B C D E
173 A B C D E
174 A B C D E
175 A B C D E

T F
176 A B C D E
177 A B C D E
178 A B C D E
179 A B C D E
180 A B C D E
181 A B C D E
182 A B C D E
183 A B C D E
184 A B C D E
185 A B C D E
186 A B C D E
187 A B C D E
188 A B C D E
189 A B C D E
190 A B C D E
191 A B C D E
192 A B C D E
193 A B C D E
194 A B C D E
195 A B C D E
196 A B C D E
197 A B C D E
198 A B C D E
199 A B C D E
200 A B C D E

Made in the USA
San Bernardino, CA
24 June 2016